Born into the CHILDREN OF GOD

My life in a religious sex cult
and my struggle for survival
on the outside

NATACHA TORMEY
WITH NADENE GHOURI

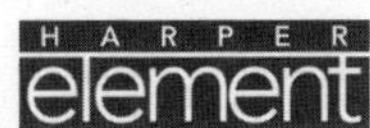

HarperElement
An imprint of HarperCollins*Publishers*
77–85 Fulham Palace Road,
Hammersmith, London W6 8JB

www.harpercollins.co.uk

and HarperElement are trademarks of
HarperCollins*Publishers* Ltd

First published by HarperElement 2014

1 3 5 7 9 10 8 6 4 2

A catalogue record of this book is
available from the British Library

ISBN 978-0-00-756032-5

Printed and bound in Great Britain by
Clays Ltd, St Ives plc

MIX
Paper from
responsible sources
FSC® C007454

Contents

	Acknowledgements	vii
	Family Tree	viii
	Berg's Household	ix
Prologue	Ants Are Bitter	xi
Chapter 1	Moonlight and Star	1
Chapter 2	God's Whores	10
Chapter 3	Fairytales and Thunderbolts	21
Chapter 4	Dances for the King	32
Chapter 5	Terror in the Shed	43
Chapter 6	Candles and Confessions	53
Chapter 7	Torn Apart	65
Chapter 8	Ruled by Fear	74
Chapter 9	From Russia with Love	88
Chapter 10	Mutiny at Tea	103
Chapter 11	Walking with Buffaloes	118
Chapter 12	The Devil's Land	127
Chapter 13	Stirrings	138
Chapter 14	A New Wine	148
Chapter 15	Changing Tides	157

Chapter 16	Happy New End Time	166
Chapter 17	A Door Opens	175
Chapter 18	A Caged Bird	181
Chapter 19	The Urban Jungle	194
Chapter 20	The Prince Is Dead	206
Chapter 21	Reincarnation	219
Chapter 22	The Woman in the Mirror	229
Epilogue	Buckinghamshire, 2014	243
	Author's Note	255

Acknowledgements

To my co-author, Nadene Ghouri, thank you for your hard work and commitment to this project. With your help my story has been brought to life and I am glad I had someone to share this journey with.

To my wonderful husband, thank you for encouraging me to face up to my past. Without your love I could not have found the immense happiness I feel today.

This book is the story of my past, based on what I saw and experienced in my childhood. It was not written with malicious intent, but as part of my road to recovery. I hope that by sharing it I will help raise awareness of the long-lasting effects a cult upbringing can have on an individual.

In order to protect the identity of my loved ones I have changed names, places and personal information.

Family Tree

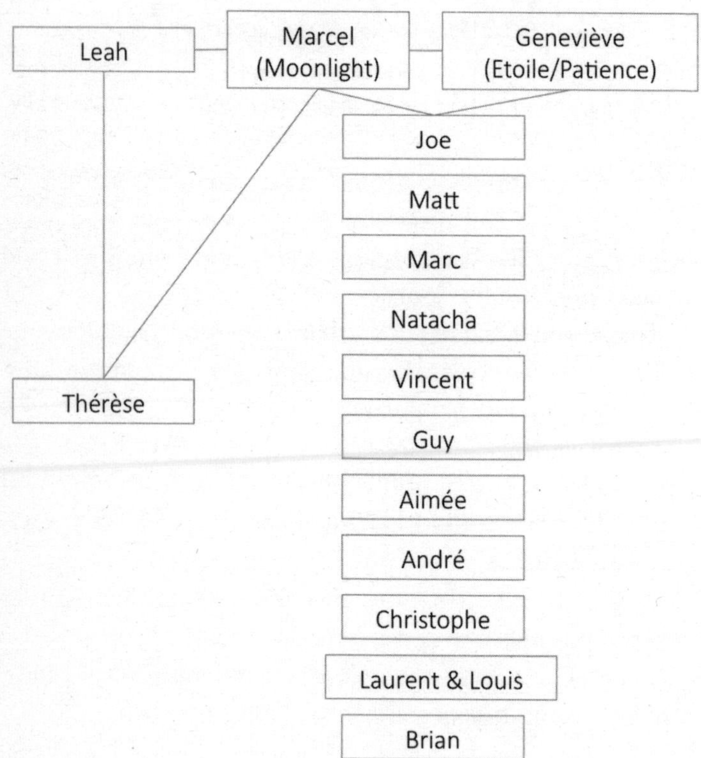

Leah
Marcel
(Moonlight)
Geneviève
(Etoile/Patience)
Thérèse
Joe
Matt
Marc
Natacha
Vincent
Guy
Aimée
André
Christophe
Laurent & Louis
Brian

Berg's Household

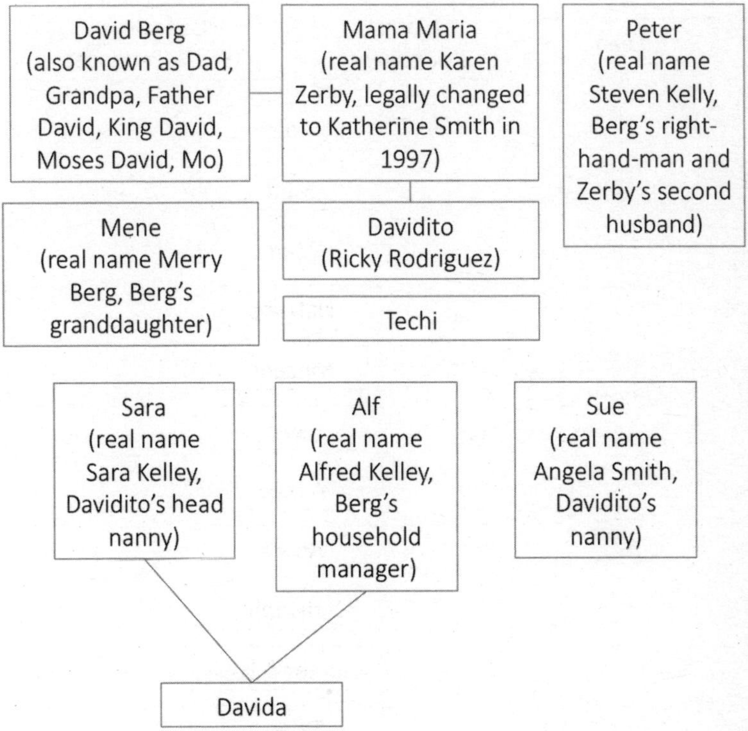

David Berg
(also known as Dad, Grandpa, Father David, King David, Moses David, Mo)

Mama Maria
(real name Karen Zerby, legally changed to Katherine Smith in 1997)

Peter
(real name Steven Kelly, Berg's right-hand-man and Zerby's second husband)

Mene
(real name Merry Berg, Berg's granddaughter)

Davidito
(Ricky Rodriguez)

Techi

Sara
(real name Sara Kelley, Davidito's head nanny)

Alf
(real name Alfred Kelley, Berg's household manager)

Sue
(real name Angela Smith, Davidito's nanny)

Davida

Prologue
Ants Are Bitter

The hot acidic smell stung my nostrils and caught in the back of my throat.

I badly needed to cough. I knew showing any revulsion would result in violence, so I forced myself to take short stabbing breaths through my mouth.

Uncle Isaiah squatted low over the campfire, tossing a heavy metal frying pan back and forth over the flames. A horrible smell floated up from his ingredients. Half a dozen of us children sat in a circle in a small clearing cut from the dense jungle of tropical ferns and leafy plants. We had our legs crossed and our backs ramrod straight, as he had ordered. Tall trees in the canopy towered over us, blocking out the breeze and concentrating the smell.

My younger brother Vincent sat next to me. I could sense his body tensing but I dared not risk turning to look at him. I glanced at the kids opposite, checking their reactions. They stared at the ground or straight ahead, expressions compliant in the mask of submission we had all learned to perfect. They didn't fool me. I knew they were thinking the same thing as me: *How am I going to keep them down?*

Earlier, Uncle had shown us how to make fire by rubbing sticks together. He seemed to enjoy seeing us struggle. My hands were sore and blistered from trying. Eventually the fire had ignited, and I felt very proud of myself as I watched orange flames lick at the heavy branches we had cut down and carried through thick bush. It was late afternoon but the temperature was still searing, made even hotter by sitting so close to the fire. Isaiah was crouched over with his back to me. Stubby, hairy legs poked from his khaki shorts, making me think of the scary spiders that ran out from under our beds when we swept the dormitory.

It was April and the start of the monsoon season in Malaysia. My muddy denim dungarees and baggy T-shirt stuck to me.

The jungle terrified me. I glanced over my shoulder to see if I could make out pairs of glowing eyes in the bushes, imagining that at any second a venomous snake might bite me or a snarling tiger would leap from the trees and seize me in its massive jaws. Swarms of buzzing mosquitoes surrounded us like a hive of bees, diving at my head in waves of assault. I had itchy red bites all along my arms; trying to swat them away was useless.

Uncle Isaiah stood up with a grin of triumph, the pan clutched in his hand. He looked over at the assembled group.

He got angry very quickly. So when he held out the frying pan and gestured to us to come and inspect it we did as we were told.

Several huge black ants sizzled in the bottom.

They gave off a sickening, chemical smell that hurt my nose. Most were dead and crispy, but a few were still alive, wriggling their spindly legs in a desperate bid to escape the heat.

'Take,' he ordered in a thick Irish brogue.

I tried very hard not to let him see me wince as I gingerly picked up a few ants, trying to avoid any that were still alive or burning my fingers on the hot pan.

'Eat,' he ordered.

I hesitated for a split second but the look on Uncle's face was stern. I took a deep breath, put the ants in my mouth and gulped. I could feel their legs tickling my throat. I felt the vomit rise up. I took a big gulp and swallowed it back down along with the ants.

They were so bitter, so completely disgusting. Yet not a single child failed to eat a handful. My brother Vincent even managed to lie: 'Mmmm, ants are delicious.'

Clearly happy with us, Uncle smiled. I knew this was all for our own good, so that we grew up brave enough to be allowed our superpowers. But I so hoped his smile meant the lesson was over and we could go home to bed. We had been marching through trees or collecting wood for hours, and my limbs were aching and sore.

His next instruction made me weep inside.

'Next we learn how to fry grasshoppers. Go find some and bring them back for the pan.'

Without a word we did as we were told.

Half an hour later I was munching on a crispy fried grasshopper. They weren't too bad – kind of nutty.

Chapter 1

Moonlight and Star

It was the famously sweltering summer of 1976, with the hottest recorded weather conditions in Europe since meteorological records began. The Cold War between the United States and the Soviets was at its height. The arms race dominated the news, with the omnipresent threat of a nuclear Armageddon giving kids nightmares. On the radio, Queen's 'Bohemian Rhapsody', Abba's 'Dancing Queen' and the Carpenters' 'There's a Kind of Hush' dominated the airwaves. The hippy counter-culture movement that had begun in the late 1960s began to lose out in popularity to disco and glam rock, but not before the hippy ideals had swept up hundreds of thousands of youths around the world desperate to throw off the shackles of their parents' more conservative post-war generation.

Against this backdrop, in the beautiful bohemian city of Paris, a roguishly handsome 20-year-old Frenchman called Marcel lived in a shared house along with several other young hippies. The housemates were an eclectic lot, from all over the world and from lots of different backgrounds. What they had in common was a hatred of established convention, a desire not to work for a living and a fervent faith in Jesus.

They passed their days in a euphoric blur of guitar strumming, tambourine shaking, folk singing and pounding the streets of Paris trying to persuade others to share their faith.

That afternoon, Marcel had walked along the river Seine, attempting to sell radical Christian pamphlets which warned of the end of the world to bemused passers-by. Marcel believed the Antichrist was everywhere, busily plotting the downfall of a human race too stupid to realise it. His warnings were genuinely heartfelt and passionate, but to the hot and bothered grey-suited commuters more concerned with catching the next metro home after a long day at the office, he was a weirdo.

By the end of the day he had sold only a handful of pamphlets, earning just a few francs. He was only allowed to keep 10 per cent of that to buy food for the day; the rest of his takings went to his overseer – a kind of manager. He looked despondently at the coins in his hand and decided, despite being extremely thirsty, that he didn't have enough to buy a cold drink. 'Get the victory, Marcel, get the victory,' he repeated to himself determinedly, before heading off down another boulevard.

As the rush hour ended and the streets emptied out, he saw no point in staying and headed for home, hoping for a lie down. But it wasn't to be. His overseer was in the hallway waiting for him. Unsmiling, the man handed Marcel a smart shirt and trousers and ordered him to change out of his T-shirt and red velvet bell-bottoms. Perplexed, Marcel did as he was told. Next the overseer told him to go into a quiet side room and write out a report detailing his movements throughout the day as well as admitting to any wicked or impure thoughts he'd had.

Two hours later he was still sitting in the room wondering why. He didn't dare leave without permission but he had no idea why he was there in the first place. He was getting nervous.

Eventually the man came back. Stony-faced, he ushered Marcel into the main living room. As Marcel entered he saw all of his housemates standing in a circle. They began cheering and clapping. Marcel felt a rush of relief that he clearly wasn't in trouble, but he still had no idea what was going on.

A beautiful green-eyed woman wearing a long cotton dress walked out from behind the circle. A ring of daisies crowned hair that fell to her waist like a golden waterfall. The overseer broke into a huge grin, clapped him on the back and announced the evening's entertainment.

Marcel was my dad and the beautiful woman my mom, Geneviève. It was to be their wedding.

And that, without warning, was how their life together began.

The shared house Marcel lived in belonged to the Children of God, an evangelical Christian cult which later changed its name to The Family of Love, or The Family. My mother, who was 18 at the time of her marriage, had been a member for just a few months. My father had joined three years earlier, when he was 17.

The group was founded and led by David Berg, an evangelical preacher's son from California. The Children of God were unashamedly Christian but also tapped into the hippy anti-establishment zeitgeist of free love, East/West spiritualism and philosophy. That mixed-up combination was popular at the time, and Berg wasn't the only well-known spiritual guru to emerge in those years. Berg was, as successful gurus always are, a charismatic and powerful orator with the ability to influence others. He was also a sexual predator who liked his disciples to send him videos of themselves having orgies. He preached that Jesus was a man who liked sex, therefore it was not something to be ashamed of.

Across the USA and Europe, tens of thousands of young hippies like my parents eagerly signed up to the Children of God, believing the group represented the greater good – love, freedom, peace and a desire to save the world.

My mom and dad didn't know it then, but their wedding day was just a taster of how the group would go on to define every single aspect of their lives in future. And of mine.

My dad had a very tough upbringing. Family life was difficult for him because his family was very poor. But he did well at school and was the first person in his family expected to go to university.

His elder brother, Frederique, had encountered a Children of God commune in Switzerland whilst on a long hiking trip. He regaled his younger brother with his adventures. The teenage Marcel was stifled by country life and desperate for a way out. His brother's tales had opened his eyes to the possibility of a much wider and more exciting world, and school no longer seemed as interesting.

Then he met a group of travelling musicians in Toulouse. They weren't much older than him but they were funny and full of life. They invited him to join them for dinner. He was overwhelmed with their warmth and concern for him. When they told him they belonged to a group called the Children of God he remembered the stories Frederique had told him about the fun he'd had staying at their Swiss commune. The next day, when the musicians checked out, he asked if he could tag along. They whooped and hugged him.

A day later he found himself in the bustling capital city of Paris, where the Children of God had their French headquarters. The group had grown in number very rapidly from its inception in California in 1968 and now boasted thousands of young members from all around the world. They included the parents of actor brothers River and Joaquin Phoenix and the parents of Hollywood actress Rose McGowan. Even the celebrities of the day joined up. One of the most famous bands of that time was Fleetwood Mac. After playing a live concert one night guitarist Jeremy Spencer suddenly disappeared without telling his bandmates. Some Children of God devotees had been in his audience, and after talking to them for a while he had joined up that same night, cutting his long hair and renouncing all his material wealth.

In the French HQ lived 200 under-25s. They were well organised, with song and dance troupes whose job it was to spread the word and raise funds. People slept several to a room and referred to each other as brother and sister, giving my dad an instant sense of kinship. Girls floated around in flowing skirts and translucent tunics (those were the days when young women burned or threw off their bras as a political statement). In the group, females were encouraged to be free and without inhibition. For the lost and lonely country boy this new life was nothing short of a revelation. When it was explained to him that followers were expected to cut off all ties with their biological families in order to devote themselves to the group, he had no qualms whatsoever. The Children of God were his family now, and he couldn't have been happier about it.

The group had a very strict no drugs or drink rule. Instead followers were encouraged to 'get high on Jesus'.

A few weeks after arriving in Paris, Marcel received the news that his brother Frederique was dead. About a year earlier Frederique had been committed to an asylum. In those days they could be brutal places where doctors often tested out experimental drugs or treatments, like lobotomies, on patients. Frederique had been unable to survive this torture. He had escaped through a barred window and killed himself by jumping into a quarry. They found his body three days later. For Marcel this was tragic news.

He was baptised shortly afterwards within the cult and renamed Moonlight.

All new recruits were expected take part in several hours of Bible study each day. They read the New Testament and took part in 'inspiration' classes, where disciples sang, danced and gave out group hugs. They even had a special term for the hugs – love bombing.

At the weekends they went out with more experienced group members who taught them how to raise funds by selling flyers or begging for donations. They also went on evangelical road trips to different cities to preach the word of God. On these trips they were encouraged to 'live by faith', which basically meant not spending any money and attempting to solicit free meals and lodging. More often than not they didn't have much success and would find themselves huddled up in their thin sleeping bags in freezing basements or car parks. Most thought that this was all incredibly exciting.

Whatever funds they did raise they were expected to bring back to the group. Only a maximum of 10 per cent could be set aside for subsistence. That meant if they raised 100 French francs a day, only 10 francs went towards their food.

Children of God leader David Berg was at this time based in California, but he very quickly became a huge influence on his young followers overseas. They were encouraged to read Berg's prolific writings, known as Mo letters, and to listen to his tape-recorded sermons. He became a role model, almost like a parent, who gave his disciples guidance and advice about life.

Mostly, Berg's writings were a treatise on the evils of the 'system' world – governments, corporations and people who had jobs. Berg claimed to be a prophet, saying God had personally given him a message, which foretold the end of the world. The End Time Tribulation, as it was known, would be marked by a series of wars and natural disasters. He used the threat of nuclear war and imminent global financial crisis to back this up. To a naïve hippy like Marcel this was all too easy to swallow. Berg promised his followers that when the End Time came they would be God's Chosen Warriors at the battle of Armageddon. They would fight the Antichrist in the skies and be the saviours of a new, more peaceful world. He backed it up with a series of sci-fi-style posters depicting the fight. Antichrist soldiers in grey uniforms and helmets zapping scantily clad young women into oblivion before they float up to a heavenly paradise, their faces ecstatic with joy.

His young devotees lapped it all up, whipping their tambourines to new heights of frenzy as they hung onto his every word.

Marcel was a fast and enthusiastic learner, carrying out each new task with a joyful smile on his face. His eagerness to please caught the attention of the French leadership, and after a few months he was given the responsibility of leading a small fundraising team. At the end of each month all funds raised within the house were totalled up, less the 10 per cent spent on evangelism costs. Half of what was left was kept back to pay for the house bills – food, heating and clothes. The other 50 per cent was posted to Berg's headquarters. No one questioned why this was.

New recruits – meaning new mouths to feed – arrived all the time. When supplies fell low followers were simply instructed to pray, and if they went without they were told they hadn't prayed hard enough.

After a year or so my dad was promoted again, this time to Home Shepherd, meaning he was responsible for ensuring the good behaviour (no alcohol, drugs or sex) of his house-mates. He was charming and popular, but he could be stern and command respect when needed, so he excelled in this new role.

He climbed the ladder even higher at the age of 19 by reaching the rank of Regional Shepherd. His role was like that of a roving manager, creating new communes in different towns and leading a musical troupe around the country singing folk songs in restaurants, schools and old people's homes. He was expected to spread himself across several different communes, often hundreds of kilometres apart. The group didn't provide vehicles or pay for transport, so he had to hitchhike everywhere. He often arrived at a house after days of travelling and sleeping rough to find himself bedded down in a corridor or on a cold kitchen floor. But he didn't care because for the first time in his life he had a purpose. The fact that Children of God missionaries were young beautiful people who seemed to love their life and exude a sense of fun and passion meant it wasn't too hard for them to win over others. Marcel would tell anyone who listened how God and the group had saved him from a life of despair. Every recruit he brought in was seen as a soul saved and another brownie point for him in the eyes of the leadership. His ascent through the ranks seemed assured.

In the early summer of 1976, Marcel was leading a team of four 'on the road' disciples. They had hitchhiked across the west coast of France, busking in bars and selling the 'prophet's messages' – pamphlets written by David Berg. By now Berg's stature had grown, so much so that his followers referred to him as either Moses David, King David or Father David.

One of Marcel's team members left due to ill health so he requested that the leadership find him a replacement.

Earlier that spring he had gone to a training centre for new recruits in the city of Bordeaux to stock up on boxes of pamphlets. As the troupe performed a few songs a new 'babe', 18-year-old Geneviève, danced for them. Marcel found her alluring but, wary of breaking the rules, he held back. Luckily, she was to be his new team member.

The pair soon fell in love.

Chapter 2

God's Whores

'I want to play! Let me. They won't let me play. Mommy, tell them!' I stamped my feet in the sand and stuck my bottom lip so far out it could catch flies.

'Who, *ma chérie*? What's the matter?' smiled my mother absently from where she was sitting on a blanket tending to my baby half-sister, Thérèse. She didn't look up but continued to blow big fat raspberry kisses on the baby's face, causing her to gurgle with pleasure. Seeing that added jealousy to my anger.

'Them,' I yelled, pointing angrily at my elder brothers who were jumping up and down on a driftwood log, pretending it was a pirate ship. 'They won't let me play with them.'

'So play something else, Natacha,' she replied without taking her gaze from the baby.

I let out a grunt of rage. Even at the age of three I had a real temper when I didn't get my way. Leah was sitting next to my mother. She cocked an eyebrow at me and when I glared back at her she burst out laughing indulgently. I ran to her across the sand, throwing myself onto her lap, burying my head into her soft bosom and wrapping my little fingers around her frizzy curls.

God's Whores

Leah was baby Thérèse's mother and my father's lover. Thérèse was his child. They lived with us in our new home, a group commune in Phuket, Thailand, that we shared with 20 or so other adults and kids. The whole group was my family but within that I had my dad, my mom, Leah, three big brothers and baby Thérèse. The set-up might have been unusual but to me it was completely normal, with the added bonus that I had two mommies when most little girls only got one.

A couple of years after my parents' surprise wedding, David Berg had instructed followers to 'hit the road' and go find new souls to save.

My parents, who by then had my elder brother Joe, took him at his word. They joined forces with three other young families to travel the country in a convoy of battered caravans. Their mission was to give 'a final warning to France' before the Antichrist took control. They were pretty much left to their own devices and had a lot of fun thinking up shock tactics. They saw themselves as evangelical commandos, invading church services and shouting at the stunned congregation that the world was about to end. To survive financially they went back to performing music in bars, with my dad playing the guitar and my mother singing. Mom, who was known as Etoile (French for 'star'), admits that these weren't the best conditions to raise a small child in, especially when dragging a tearful baby into a church invasion. Yet this was the life they had willingly chosen, and it was one they enjoyed. They were deliriously happy together.

But both were experimental young people who didn't hold any truck with conventional ideas about marital fidelity. After one gig they picked up Leah, a pretty young hippy, and took her back to their caravan. Leah never left. There was no risk of censure because the group had recently relaxed the rules on relationships by declaring that consensual threesomes and sexual swinging were allowed. Homosexuality was strictly banned, but in a reflection of his own sexual fantasies leader David Berg said it was OK for women to have sex with other women in threesomes as long as they weren't lesbians and still preferred men. They had also changed their name from the Children of God to The Family, in part to reflect their new approach to sex and relationships. It goes without saying that for Leah the deal for joining the relationship was joining The Family too.

For two years the three of them travelled round France, enduring cold winters and tough times, but generally loving both life and each other.

My mother gave birth twice more, to Matt in July 1980 and Marc in November '81. She was just 23 when Marc was born. She had always loved little babies and found each pregnancy thrilling. Her dance training meant she was extremely fit, so she coped easily.

My dad was less sure of how to behave as a parent. Luckily, as he saw it, King David (Berg) gave a lot of advice about parenting and how to raise kids. What pleased my dad was that King David never insisted someone should do what he said, instead he only offered advice through his regular Mo letters. But the letters made it clear that a true believer should indeed naturally want to do as he suggested.

Berg had four children of his own and lived with a harem of lovers, whom he called wives, at his base. His favourite lover was Maria, known to followers as Mama Maria. He claimed to have a series of spirit helpers who possessed his body and handed down God's prophecies. His most common helper was Abrahim – an ancient gypsy king who demanded wine before making his revelations. In several of the Mo letters of this time Maria is questioning Abrahim as he (really Berg) demands more alcohol. In one dated from 1978, Abrahim the spirit is apparently promising he 'knows everything' and will tell 'everything you want to know' if only he is allowed one more sip of wine.

Yet for ordinary members drinking was still very much frowned upon.

As the winter of 1981 approached, my parents couldn't face staying in the caravan any longer. Life had become almost impossible with three adults and the little boys all jostling for space.

King David had decreed that his followers, who now numbered close to 10,000, should move to the 'fertile lands of the East'. He explained that these countries were less corrupt and it was easier to find souls to save. There was also the added advantage of less intrusive governments allowing large communes to operate unhindered. My mom and dad immediately volunteered to go and were sent to a farmhouse in southern France for special training.

While they were there the dictates around sex and marriage changed again. King David began promoting the 'Law of Love' – something mentioned in the Bible to mean that what is done in love is good. Berg's version was more to do with physical sex, what he called 'sharing'. He sent out new Mo letters stating it wasn't fair that single members should feel lonely and unloved. His solution was for married couples to agree to 'share' their partners by allowing them to sleep with other cult members of the opposite sex. Women especially were encouraged to willingly submit to sex if it was a way of helping someone.

When my parents first heard the rationale behind it they were surprised but not offended. King David explained that it would promote humility and unselfishness, and give a person a closer connection with God.

Another new idea was 'flirty fishing' (or FF'ing), where female followers were told to go to bars and pick men up for sex with the intent of either converting them to the cause or bringing in a financial donation. FF'ers were told they were 'God's whores'. Posters with instructions on how to be a 'good flirty little fishy' were distributed. One image depicted a naked woman wriggling on a fishing hook with the words *Hooker for Jesus*. Another depicted a woman sitting at a table with a man she is attempting to fish along with the words, *If they fall in love with you first before they find it's the Lord, it's just God's bait to hook them!*

The method was so successful that The Family also encouraged women to sign up to escort agencies in order to guarantee fixed payment for sexual services. Some members were worried because they feared the FF'ing might put women at risk of rape or violence. Sharing with men they knew was one thing; picking up strangers alone in a bar was another. King David happily admitted violence might happen but said women should accept it, comparing 'our gals' to early Christian martyrs who had been raped by Roman soldiers.

Contraception was strictly banned. At one point Berg sent out a Mo letter advising people to look out for the symptoms of common STDs, like crabs and herpes, because there had been a mass breakout.

But if a few dissented from all this, the majority accepted it without question. Berg's power base was growing. By now the group had 1,642 communes all across the world. Between them they claimed to distribute a staggering 30 million pages a month of literature produced by the cult.

In early 1982 my parents and Leah were sent to their new mission destination, a commune in the city of Phuket in Thailand. None of them had left France before, so this was an epic adventure.

It was there in September 1983 that I was born, a much-longed-for first daughter. A year later Leah gave birth to Thérèse.

My dad's Regional Shepherd role had transferred with him to Thailand, and as such he was hardly ever at home. The Family-related business generally kept him in Bangkok. My brothers missed him and cried for him a lot, but Mom told them to be proud, not sad.

I recall little of those very early years except for that one day out on the beach with my mother, brothers and Leah. I think I remember it so clearly because it is the only family day out we ever had.

I don't know how Mom managed to persuade the house overseer to let us go to the beach – it certainly wasn't usual. But I do clearly remember the sense of excitement as we helped her to pack water, bread and fruit for our picnic. As we walked down the driveway and out of the gate I remember feeling very special and hoping the other kids were watching me.

As we waited for the bus my pride turned to abject fear. System people were everywhere. They looked normal but I knew they weren't; they even dressed differently to us. As we boarded the bus the driver smiled at me and I started to howl. I thought he might be the Antichrist, driving us straight into hell, because in my child's brain anyone who wasn't part of our group was pretty much the devil.

As the rickety old bus traversed busy traffic lanes with honking horns, motorbikes and rickshaws, I could not have been more terrified. The other passengers were local Thais who found white Europeans a funny novelty. Back then Thailand wasn't the popular tourist destination it is today. Women kept ruffling our hair and making clucking noises at us in their strange language. I recoiled every time someone touched me. My mom seemed oblivious to the danger we might be in and was smiling at people. At one point she even handed over some Christian leaflets to a young couple sitting near the front. 'God loves you,' she told them, bathing them with a beautiful smile. I was so confused. Why did she do that when she knew the system people wanted to hurt us?

The ten-minute journey was unbearable, but when the bus pulled up opposite the beach I gasped with wonder at the sight of the sparkling blue water. I'd never seen the sea before because we never left the compound, except on a few occasions when I was dressed up and paraded before the public as a cute money-making machine for fund-raising.

Joe was first off the bus, hollering, 'Come on, let's run.'

The others sprinted off after him. I forgot my fears and chased behind. The hot sand burned the soles of my feet but I loved the grittily soft sensation between my toes.

We had spent a blissful day making sandcastles and eating our sandwiches until my brothers upset me by refusing to let me play pirates with them. As I sat on Leah's lap, sobbing with fury, she quietly held me until I calmed. She chastised my brothers for being so mean to me, something that made me smile triumphantly.

Joe, already well versed in the assumption that women were second class and subservient to men, shrugged. 'She's a girl, so she can't play a boys' game.'

Leah and my mother were complete opposites. Even in her missionary uniform of baggy T-shirt, long skirt and no bra, Mom still held herself like the elegant prima ballerina she had almost been. Having kids had barely affected her slender body and she still wore her hair flowing to the waist, the same way she had since her teens. In contrast, Leah was voluptuous, with frizzy hair and piercing turquoise eyes.

Their personalities were just as distinct. My mother was serene to the point of detachment. She had recently been renamed Patience, replacing her earlier given name of Etoile. Patience suited her because she was genuinely submissive and willing to play second fiddle to her husband. That was what she believed Jesus wanted from her.

Leah was more outspoken and a confident, playful joker. She was very affectionate with me and my brothers, forever scooping us up into her arms and smothering our faces with kisses. I was in no doubt that Geneviève/Etoile/Patience was my main mother but I loved Leah just as much.

I felt another pang of jealously as Leah gently lifted me off her lap and picked up Thérèse. 'Isn't she the sweetest, prettiest baby in the world?'

'She certainly is, isn't she?' my mother sang back in a silly song voice. 'Yes she is, she is, she is.'

Both of them cooed over the baby as if she was the most amazing thing they'd ever laid eyes on. It might sound odd that my mom was so rapt by a child her husband had with another woman, but that was not how she saw it. Leah was her best friend and she was closer to Leah than my father was. At times it wasn't easy but their friendship always won the day and got them through any tough patches.

With the leadership's consent, many of the overseas communes provided high-class escort services to high-ranking officials, police and businessmen. It didn't always involve sex; sometimes it was just about accompanying the men to events as arm trophies. After all, the cult included a variety of beautiful women from across the globe. From Europeans to Asians to African-Americans and Latinos – there was something to suit all tastes and fantasies, and for the cult it made perfect business sense. Escorting certainly brought funds in but it also served as a convenient way of ensuring local authorities didn't ask too many questions about the group's wider activities. I remember watching as the ladies would get dressed up to go out at night. Normally they looked so plain in their baggy everyday clothes, but as they got ready and put on fancy dresses and make-up they were, in my eyes at least, transformed into magnificent birds of paradise.

I was a very teary child at that time. Going to bed terrified me and I would often scream and cry. It was usually left to Leah or another 'aunty' to calm me. We were meant to be one big family so we referred to all other adults as aunties and uncles. Any adult was allowed to discipline any child as they wished – it didn't matter if they weren't that child's actual parents. I made such a racket that people became very impatient with me. If Leah hadn't been there to protect me I am sure I would have been treated much more harshly.

A part of my dad's job was to match women – other men's wives – for sharing. My dad insists most people did it willingly and no one was forced into it if they didn't want to do it. But in an atmosphere where not going along with things led to accusations of being unspiritual, a doubter or what was called a 'backslider', it was very hard to say no. Dad insists he always tried to make people happy with it, aiming to match people he knew liked each other anyway. Only once did a woman refuse to be part of his sharing schedule, and that was because she was five months' pregnant. Women were supposed to share at up to eight months but this woman didn't think she should have to.

'King David' had also declared that 12 was the age when a child reached adult maturity, essentially setting the framework for young girls to be forced into sex. He wrote about the importance of teenage marriages, saying Jesus had blessed them so they should be encouraged. He had already published a pamphlet called 'The Little Girl Dream', which depicted a cartoon likeness of himself and his lover, Maria, in bed with a pre-pubescent girl. Within the cult literature he was normally depicted in animation, with a long beard and wearing robes. On the rare occasions that a real photograph of him was published it always had a cartoon lion's head drawn over it, completely obscuring his face. We were told this was to help protect him because if the Antichrist knew what he really looked like it would risk his safety. In reality he was cautious because he was fully aware some of his publications could be deemed immoral or illegal by outsiders, whom he referred to as 'systemites'. Several of his books and Mo letters came with the instruction 'BAR', burn after reading.

But, as ever, nothing he wrote was a 'must-do', rather a 'should-do'. As such, my dad says he didn't match 12-year-olds under his watch and that he doesn't recall any other local leaders in Thailand doing so either. Different communes around the world had different norms, and thankfully, in Thailand at least, this bit of depravity didn't seem to be standard practice.

Chapter 3

Fairytales and Thunderbolts

I was fast asleep when I felt something tickle my face, waking me up. It took me a second to register what was happening as the thing ran right across my cheeks, scratching me with sharp little toes.

I screamed out in terror. 'Arrrggggh. Moooommm-mmmy'.

My yelling woke the others. I shared my bedroom with four other girls under the age of ten. 'Natacha, be quiet,' snapped my friend Anna who was sleeping in the bunk above me. She leaned over to chastise me, but as she looked down her eyes fell on what had made me scream. Her mouth opened in horror for a split second before she started yelling too. A brown lizard stared back at us, probably more terrified than we were. It ran for cover under the bunk, making me scream even louder: 'MOMMY! HELP!'

The door flew open. My brother Matt stood there with an exasperated look on his face. 'Natacha, what is this racket?'

Great gulping sobs came out as I tried to explain: 'Lizard … bed … it was … on me … want … my … mommy.'

Matt sighed and shook his head at me with annoyance. 'Cry baby. Mom is out. It's only a silly lizard.'

He disappeared for a second and came back with a broom. He poked it under the bed, ordering the lizard to shoo. I watched with relief as it slithered out of the door and down the corridor, no doubt to join the rest of its friends in the attic where they nested.

I was just about to throw my arms around my big brother in thanks when the shape of adult bulk appeared in the doorway. Uncle Ezekiel. He was a heavy-set Australian man and probably the meanest uncle in our house.

'What in God's name is going on here? You children could wake the dead. Get back to sleep immediately or you will get a spanking, mark my words.'

'There was a lizard,' Matt tried to explain. 'It scared them. They are only little. We should do something about that nest.'

Ezekiel stared at Matt with a look of disgust.

'How dare you speak to me, boy. I was not talking to you. Nor did I give you permission to talk to me. Get out!'

He raised his fist in warning. Matt ducked under his arm and ran out.

'We are sorry, Uncle. We promise it won't happen again,' said Sara.

'It had better not or you will get the swat. Do you understand?'

I pulled my sheet up to my chin and nodded with wide-eyed fear. The swat was a plastic fly-swatter, which was used to discipline us when we were naughty. You got hit on the bare bottom with the handle and it stung like mad.

Uncle closed the door. I could hear Anna and the other kids breathing. I could tell they were still awake but no one dared talk in case Uncle heard us and came back. Our teacher, Aunty Joy, usually slept in the room with us. Her presence always reassured me, but tonight her bed was empty. I wondered if she was upstairs in Ezekiel's room or if she'd gone flirty fishing with Mommy and the other ladies.

I tried to go back to sleep but it was too stuffy and the polyester sheets itched. I was terrified the lizard would climb inside my mouth or my ears when I was asleep. I was also bursting for a pee but I knew that if anyone heard me I would get the swat for sure. Under the commune rules, children were expected to last a full night without needing the toilet. I tossed and turned half the night, trying desperately to control my bladder and not wet the bed.

The next morning in school I could hardly keep my eyes open. We sat at rows of little wooden chairs and desks. Children of all ages shared the one large classroom, with the little kids at the front and the older kids at the back. A small fan buzzed in the corner but the windows were closed, allowing precious little breeze into the stifling tropical atmosphere. Everyone was quietly reading on their own, with the older kids occasionally pausing to scribble down a note. The quiet, the lack of sleep and the heat made my eyelids heavy. I could feel my chin about to droop down onto my chest when Aunty Joy's voice startled me: 'Natacha, wake up please, little lady.'

I sprang to attention, sitting bolt upright on my chair with arms folded tightly across my chest. Aunty Joy pulled up a seat and sat down next to me. Her youthful Thai features erupted into a pretty smile that lit up her face. Joy was my favourite teacher.

'Natacha, I have something very special for you to read today.'

She handed me a large comic book, wrinkling her nose with excitement. The humidity made its greying pulp pages feel slightly moist to touch. I stared at the cover. It had a picture of a pretty young teenage girl with lustrous long black hair in a braid. Aunty Joy began to sound out the title for me.

'He … van … s. Can you say that?' beamed Joy.

'Hev …' I stammered, struggling to match the letters she pointed to with the correct sounds.

The next word was easy. I could guess its meaning from the picture.

'Girl,' I said triumphantly.

'Well done, Natacha, you clever girl.'

A thrill ran through me as I looked at the image.

'Do you want to read it together, Natacha?' she asked.

I nodded so hard I thought my head might fall off. I rarely got individual adult attention and was determined to milk this for all it was worth. My clammy fingers fumbled with the thin paper as I opened it several pages into the story. A girl dressed in a short white robe was throwing two men backwards as if using magic. Her robe was see-through and her nipples stuck out through her dress. I was a bit fascinated by that because a couple of days earlier a visiting uncle had shown us a poster of another lady with similar sticky-out nipples and told us that nipples were his favourite thing in the world. He had grinned when he told us all little girls would grow up to have sexy nipples like the lady in the picture, too. Anna had whispered to me afterwards that the uncle was naughty to say that to us.

The men in the picture were dressed in helmets and sinister uniforms with armbands marked 666.

'What's Heaven's Girl doing, Aunty Joy?' I asked, puzzled and happy at the same time.

Joy laughed and pulled me closer to her.

'She's using her powers to fight the soldiers of the Antichrist. See, she's shooting them with lightning. What do you think that word says, Natacha?'

She pointed to the large graphic letters drawn above the image of the dying men. I shrugged.

'Zap!' said Joy.

'Zap!' I repeated back, feeling very pleased with myself. 'But Aunty Joy, why is she doing that?'

'Because she's in the End Time Army. You've heard your Grandpa David tell us about the End Time Army in his letters, haven't you?'

Of course I had. For as long as I could remember it had been drilled into me that I was an elite child soldier in God's army. Every day we were training and preparing for the End Time war, which would mark the beginning of end of the world. We were told Grandpa (which is what we children were instructed to call our leader, David Berg) had been sent a prophecy directly from God that the war would begin in 1993. My brothers assured me I would be ten by then and definitely old enough to fight.

Every day we listened to tapes of Grandpa talking to us. He explained how the Antichrist was already living on earth and making his evil plans to destroy the world. He said Europe and America were already under the devil's control but the system people who lived there didn't even know it. That's why they laughed at us. They thought we were crazy but that was because they were the stupid ones.

Grandpa's tapes also explained that when the war started, floods and earthquakes would ravage the world and a deep darkness would cover the earth. Joy showed me pictures of what this would look like. It was really sad – there were no flowers and all the buildings had been destroyed. He called this the 'great tribulation'. At the very end of the war there would be the battle of Armageddon, which is when God would fly down from the sky on his chariot. We would fight by God's side and die, and then we'd go to live in heaven.

I couldn't wait to get to heaven. Art was my favourite lesson because we got to draw heaven with crayons. I especially loved colouring in the outside walls of the heavenly city because they were made of precious stones, like rubies and emeralds, so I got to use lots of different colours. The main city was shaped like a pyramid and right in the middle of it there was a giant crystal skyscraper over 600 metres high. Aunty Joy said that was twice as high as the Empire State Building, which she explained was an important government building in America. Joy said anything wicked men could build God could do twice as well.

And there wasn't just one pearly gate like the stupid system people believed, there were twelve – three on each wall.

People didn't need to walk anywhere in this magical city, they whizzed through the air instead. And because I was going to be a glorious martyr it that meant my family would get a solid gold house on one of the top levels of the pyramid, areas reserved only for important people like us.

But absolutely the best bit about the war was that I would have a special superpower. I wanted this more than anything in the entire world. Joy promised us God would give all the children in the End Time Army an individual power when he was ready. But first we had to prove to him how brave and worthy we were.

I turned another page of the book.

Heaven's Girl had been captured and was about to be fed to some lions. She looked really worried and I was scared for her. But as Joy continued to read out loud I worked out that the nasty men had changed their minds about throwing her to the lions because they said they wanted a bite of her themselves instead. That really got me confused. Why would they want to eat her?

In thc drawing on the next page she was being held down by the soldiers. Two of them had her by the ankles, spreading her legs, while a third loosened his belt buckle.

I suddenly felt very flushed and uncomfortable.

'Aunty Joy, what are those men doing to Heaven's Girl?'

I knew what sex looked like – I'd seen the adults do it in their love-up sessions lots and lots of times – but this was different.

'Can't you see, Natacha, my dear?' said Joy. 'Look at what a wonderful example Heaven's Girl is setting for you. They want to rape her by force, but Grandpa David tells us there is no such thing as rape if we follow the true laws of nature. A woman of the Bible should submit willingly to a man and satisfy him. God created sex and he created a man's need for sex. He created woman to serve a man's need. Heaven's Girl is using this God-given opportunity to share the love of Jesus with these soldiers. She is going to love them *so* much that she will turn them back to the path of Jesus. She shares her love with a big smile and a song in her heart like all good girls should. Isn't that a beautiful thing?'

After Aunty Joy and I finished a few more pages of the book she closed it and promised we'd read some more tomorrow. I didn't really mind her taking it – that picture had made me feel a bit sick. I couldn't shake the thought of Heaven's Girl's smiling face as the soldiers did things to her. Would I have to do that when I was bigger? Would I be brave enough?

I began to feel a bit shaky so I tried to think about what always made me feel happy – what superpower was God going to give me? My brothers and I used to argue about it all the time. Was it better to be invisible or be able to run really fast? Did boys get better ones than girls? I bawled my eyes out when my brothers teased me by insisting that they did.

I was really into the idea of shooting thunderbolts from my eyes. I would practise my pose for hours, standing with my feet firmly planted one in front of the other, and trying to look as mean and scary as possible as I narrowed my eyes into my best thunderbolt death stare.

'Nap time.'

Aunty Joy's voice snapped me back to reality.

'Children, back to your room, PJs on and get on your beds, please.'

I groaned inwardly. I hated nap time. I would much rather have been allowed out to play in the garden where there was the big flame of the forest tree. The tree had big orange feathery plumes on its branches, and whenever we got a chance the other little girls and I would skip around it pretending to be princesses in a castle.

Without a word we filed back to our room, stripped down to our underwear and put on the sleeveless T-shirts that we wore as our pyjamas, before climbing onto our bunk beds. Some of the uncles had built them out of salvaged wood. The bolts holding my frame together were loose, and whenever I moved it creaked and swayed.

Uncle Ezekiel came into the room to supervise us. I hated the way he spoke through his nose.

I closed my eyes and tried to sleep, but the images of Heaven's Girl and the soldiers invaded my mind. I was always a fidgety child, and being mentally uneasy made it worse. I couldn't keep still.

'Natacha,' barked Uncle Ezekiel. I froze at my name.

Ezekiel and Aunty Joy were sharing the single bed – she was bare breasted and her hand was moving up and down under the blanket.

'Keep still. Go to sleep. All you children go to sleep. *Now.*'

I screwed my eyelids tight, willing myself to sleep, trying to ignore the squeaking and animal grunting coming from Joy's bed. I shuffled around in a bid to get comfortable.

A strong hand clamped around my forearm. Uncle Ezekiel's face was glaring at me.

'You disobedient girl. Get here now.'

He dragged me out of the bed so roughly that I fell face down onto the cold floor.

Uncle Ezekiel, now completely naked, stood over me – his penis wagging like a disapproving finger. He reached towards me and pulled down my underwear. I knew better than to struggle, instead clenching my jaw for what was to come.

The fly-swat slapped down hard across my buttocks, biting at my tender skin.

I squealed, more from shock and indignation than pain, and clenched my jaw tighter, determined not to give him the satisfaction of making me cry.

'Naughty, wicked girl,' he cried as the swat struck again. Then a third time. 'I hope you understand why I had to do that, Natacha. It was for your own benefit, because I love you. Now get into your bed and ask the Lord to forgive you.'

Tears silently rolled down my cheeks as Uncle Ezekiel shoved me roughly back onto my bed, my knickers still around my knees.

I lay still, my face pressing into the wall.

'If I catch any children not sleeping then they will get the same thing,' hissed Ezekiel, slightly out of breath.

With tears streaming I pushed my face into the pillow to wipe my snotty nose, daring not to move further. My head was throbbing and filled with images of Uncle Ezekiel cowering before me, pleading with me not to shoot him with thunderbolts from my eyes. This made me feel better, and I drifted into a fitful sleep, with pictures of Ezekiel begging for mercy.

When I woke up he was gone and Aunty Joy was smiling again.

'Come along, children, back to class for Memory Time,' she trilled in her sing-song accent.

In silence we climbed out of our beds, filed back into the classroom and took our seats at our little desks. My bottom still stung and my eyes felt puffy.

Joy had written some words on the blackboard and started to read them out loud: '*Then … shall … they … deliver … you … up … to … be … afflicted … and … shall … kill … you … and … ye … shall … be … hated … of … all … nations … for … my … name's … sake*. OK, children, Bibles open at Matthew, please. Let's all practise the verse together.'

We repeated it in unison. I couldn't say the word *afflicted*. Joy saw me struggling and laughed indulgently: 'Oh, little Natacha. *AF FLIC TED*. It means to suffer, like when you die.'

'Will I suffer when I die, Aunty Joy?' I asked her.

'Yes, of course, little one,' she cooed as if it was the most natural thing in the world.

'What if I don't want to?'

Aunty Joy laughed again, bathing me in her warm, beautiful smile.

'Little Natacha, if you are not willing to suffer and die for Jesus how will you get to heaven?'

Knowing I would die at a young age was not scary for me. It was a completely normal part of my life that was reinforced by every adult I knew, including my mom and dad. But it was the suffering bit that got to me. I would spend hours secretly worrying about it. Would it hurt? Would it be slow or quick? Would the person who killed me feel bad and say sorry or would they laugh and enjoy it?

Those thoughts often kept me awake at night.

Joy's voice snapped me back to reality. 'Very good, children. Let's do it again. *Then ... shall ... they ... deliver ... you ... up ... to ... be ... afflicted ... and ... shall ... kill ... you ... and ... ye ... shall ... be ... hated ... of ... all ... nations ... for ... my ... name's ... sake*. And again please, children.'

And on and on we repeated it. Again. And again. And again.

Chapter 4

Dances for the King

Aunty Joy had sent me to an upstairs storeroom to fetch some books. Thrilled to be out of the stifling classroom for a few brief moments, I walked as slowly as I possibly could.

At the top of the stairs I paused, wondering how I could drag the errand out even longer. I hit upon the ruse of pretending to be a princess inspecting my castle. Haughtily I practised an exaggerated princess walk, imagining that my brother's old hand-me-down jeans, which were two sizes too big and held up with a nylon belt, were in fact a beautiful ball gown with a big petticoat skirt. I pranced along, swishing my imaginary dress from side to side as I went.

The sight of a bedroom door, left ajar, stopped me hard in my make-believe tracks – one prancing leg still raised up above the floor. Why oh why hadn't I noticed it sooner? Being seen or heard by the occupants was something I really didn't want to happen.

Gingerly I put my foot down, trying to be an ever-so-quiet tiny-little mouse.

I heard the people in the room giggling.

'Who's there? Come on, nothing to be scared of. Come and say hi,' said a male voice.

I winced. Saying hi was the very last thing I wanted to do.

'Heeeellloooo?' came a female voice I recognised as Aunty Salome. She was from Minnesota in the United States and was married with one son, a few years older than me. I got the impression she didn't like children very much, so I usually tried to avoid her.

The male voice spoke again: 'Is that a demon? Or is it a little person? Is it an embarrassed little person?'

At that the pair started to giggle again, followed by a few seconds of silence before the woman let out a low little moan.

The man spoke again: 'Hey, you kids shouldn't be wandering about. Aren't you supposed to be in Word Time? I'm in no mood to come out there and chastise you so pop yourself right in here and tell me what your business is.'

The tone of his voice made it clear I didn't have much choice. Reluctantly I hovered by the entrance, trying very hard not to look inside.

'It's Natacha. Aunty Joy sent me up here to get some books from the cupboard. I have to get them and go back to my class. Sorry if I disturbed you, Aunty Salome.'

At that I turned to make my escape. But the man, amused now, was having none of it.

'Why so shy, little one? We aren't demons either. Come and say hi.'

'I really need to get back to my class. Aunty Joy said …' I trailed off nervously.

'Joy won't tell you off for being a polite little girl. One minute to say hello, that's all we are asking. You wouldn't deny your uncle and aunty that, would you?' he countered.

The woman's voice spoke back to him, slightly impatiently. 'Stop teasing her, Peter. It's putting me off.' Then she snapped to me: 'Natacha, stop being a silly girl. Show yourself like your uncle has asked you.'

I took a step into the room, still trying to avert my gaze from the bed where the two were lying. That made them laugh even harder.

'Oh my, look at her. What a little prude. Natacha, LOOK. AT. US. We don't bite.'

I lifted my head up. On the little side table next to the bed was a bottle of Dettol disinfectant spray, a big box of tissues and a candle. That's what all adults kept by their bed. I knew the Dettol and tissues were for hygiene because we kids used the same. Joy had explained to me that the candle was to help them make the room look pretty and give it a nice mood during love-ups. Lying in the bed next to Salome was a man I didn't recognise. The crumpled sheets barely covered their naked bodies.

'I am Uncle Peter,' he explained. 'I live in Bangkok. I'm just visiting. Natacha? Natacha, Natacha ... I know your name. I know your daddy, don't I? You are Shepherd Moonlight's little girl?'

I nodded.

'Ah, you are as cute as a button, just as he said you were. Well, lovely to meet you, Natacha. You had better get those books then, hadn't you?'

At that he stuck out his hand, offering it for me to shake. I didn't move.

'Come on, silly girl. I already said I don't bite. SHAKE. MY. HAND.'

I reached forward and with the merest hint of my fingertips gave him a tiny shake. He lunged towards me, making a growling noise: 'Grrrr. I fibbed. I do bite. Grrrrrrrrr. Come here little girl. Let me eat you!'

I yelped, stumbling into the table.

'Peter, quit it now. You're scaring the poor kid!' snapped Salome. 'Natacha, please don't be scared. Peter was just joking with you. He's a big silly billy, aren't you, Peter?' At that she raised herself onto her elbow and leaned over him, her breasts dangling in his face. The sight of that made him forget all about me.

'Oh, am I now, my lady? Well, maybe I am going to bite your titties. Grrrrr. Come here and let me eat YOU.'

At that the pair of them collapsed into a heap, her squealing with excited giggles, him still making the stupid roaring noise. I seized my chance and ran out.

This kind of thing was par for the course. Everywhere I looked grown-ups were having sex. They left the doors open, they had orgies in the living room, they stood kissing and groping each other in the hallways. They never made any attempt to hide it from us because they thought sexual openness was not only healthy, it was divine. Grandpa preached that love – sex – was something Jesus wanted his believers to do lots of. By being so open about it the adults weren't trying to harm us, they genuinely thought it would make us healthier adults and better Christians too. But I hated seeing it. For me, the sight of adults making out was just gross.

Grandpa was completely open about his attitude to sex and children. We were read to from a book he wrote called *The Devil Hates Sex but God Loves It*. The cover of it had a naked couple making love as God smiles over them. In it Grandpa talked about children and sex: 'How beautiful it is and how true and how Godly and how Biblical and so on, and yet how dangerous for us to even put out such a truth! I mean if you want to infuriate the system, just talk about teaching sex to children, or allowing children any sexual activities or to explore sex or anything. Whew! They've passed so many laws against sex it's almost unbelievable!'

In another letter Mama Maria wrote: 'It's pure to us, there's nothing wrong with it, so we let our kids be in on it, we let them get in on it if they want, we even play it with them because it's nice, it makes them feel good and they enjoy it.'

Masses of similar letters were sent out with the instruction BAR, burn after reading. Not all of these letters were taught to us in the classroom; others were read out during group prayer sessions where the whole house, children and adults, gathered together in the dining hall for worship. I hated these occasions, not least because I always struggled to sit still. I couldn't help but fidget, which more often than not got me a spanking.

I had a little friend called Simon who was my age. We used to hide under the stairs and have pretend sex. He would mimic exactly what he'd seen the adult men do and hump at me, pretending to penetrate me. Instead of finding it shocking the adults laughed at us. 'Ah, they are sharing already. How cute.'

Times were financially tough in the commune and our food rations were smaller than usual due to a lack of donors willing to provide us food. We ate a lot of boiled rice or mangoes, which often had maggots inside them. One of the aunties was heavily pregnant around this time. She clearly wasn't getting enough nutrients and didn't look well. She was sent on a fundraising trip in the middle of the monsoon season when it was so hot and sticky that being outdoors for even a few minutes was uncomfortable. In a crowded side street she began to miscarry. She was rushed to a filthy local clinic where she delivered a stillborn baby. When she got back, white-faced and shaking, the other adults urged her to 'get the victory', the term they used for overcoming any and all adversity.

One morning I woke up to find everyone talking in hushed tones and looking very worried. We were ushered into the dining hall and told God had sent word that the End Time was getting nearer. I felt a shiver of fear run through me. They told us agents of the Antichrist had located Grandpa's whereabouts and had made an attempt to capture him. I gasped. Grandpa was our King – the thought of people trying to hurt him was terrible.

The adults explained that if the devil's forces killed our prophet, they could destroy the army he had formed to save the world – us. Therefore Grandpa had to be protected at all costs. From now on only a few trusted aides could know where he was. What wasn't explained to us that day was that those aides were the only people, aside from Berg himself, who knew the real truth about why he needed to go into hiding. The authorities were investigating him for child abuse and suspicion of pimping.

New instructions were sent out to all communes urging us to be more cautious. Adults began to use a code of secret knocks whenever they entered a building. Anyone who went out witnessing had to telephone in before coming home again, using a secret code to gain entry. And all mail was to come in and out through secret PO boxes, which were checked twice a month in military-style operations carried out by adults in disguise. Children were given extra drills urging us not to talk to strangers or answer any questions about who we were or where we lived. We were told only to say: 'I am sorry. I don't know anything.'

Yet this didn't stop the sexual nature that defined so much of life within The Family from getting more and more depraved. In Greece the group had a large commune led by a man called Paul Peloquin. The commune's role was to produce *Music with Meaning* videos, which were used as learning tools for members.

We watched a film they had made called *Glorify God in the Dance*, in which naked pre-pubescent girls and women danced suggestively or, as it was explained to me, 'joyfully for God'. The film had originally been made as a present for Berg but he apparently loved it so much he ordered copies of it to be sent to all communes along with his advice on how each of the women and girls could be a 'dancing girl' too.

This was read out to us: 'When you rub your hands on the sides of your belly and down your crotch it's really exciting. It really is thrilling to watch a girl caress herself, very stimulating, masturbating breasts and bum with your hands!'

I can't say for sure if I took part in this but I think perhaps so, because today I have flashbacks of dancing while wearing a thin veil.

One thing I remember more vividly is the day Joy showed the class a book called *The Story of Davidito*. Like most books she showed me it didn't make a great deal of sense to me. There was a lot of very hard to understand writing and biblical quotes. But mostly the book was a series of pictures of a little boy. There he was as a baby, then walking along a path, then lying in bed with an aunty kissing him on the lips. Joy read me the words above the picture: 'When two lie together they shall have heat.'

Joy said this little boy was very important. His mommy was Maria, whom I knew was Grandpa's favourite wife. She explained how Davidito had been the very first 'Jesus baby' born to The Family, meaning Jesus had sent him to us as a gift. Davidito's father was a Spanish waiter and Maria had only one night of love with him. When she found out she was pregnant the man was not interested and disowned his child. Grandpa David offered the man all the riches of the spiritual world, Maria as his wife and a place in his home if he would only accept God's will and his little baby. But the man preferred his evil path within the system and said no.

So in an act of the highest kindness and grace, because of course as Joy explained, Grandpa was the world's nicest person, he adopted Davidito as his own son and heir.

Grandpa also decreed that more Jesus babies should be born, and this is why he invented flirty fishing – so that God could bless us all with lots of babies. She said that within our family there were at least 300 other Jesus babies who had come to us through FF'ing.

The numbers were boring me by this point but I started to listen more intently when Joy mentioned Armageddon again. This always made me serious. But whenever I got worried about it I tried to focus on the solid gold house that we would live in. I wondered what my bedroom might look like and if I would have to share it or if I would have one of my own. I was also comforted by the fact that there would be no systemite people in heaven. Given how they terrified me, this sounded very good indeed.

Joy's voice built to a crescendo as she told us Grandpa had been given a new prophecy directly from God. 'Can you guess what it said, children? I bet you can't! Can you? Try!'

'More wars?' suggested one kid. 'Jesus will give us more powers?' tried another.

Joy laughed her shiny tinkling laugh and shook her head.

'This prophecy is about the End Time itself! It is so very exciting. Davidito will be the general of our army, leading us all – and leading all of *you* – at the battle of Armageddon.'

We all stared at her blankly as she shrieked with exhilaration.

'Davidito will die and be the most glorious of all martyrs! He will fight a brave fight but he will fall in battle, brutally slain by the Antichrist himself! The Lord will lift him up and place him right by his side where he will live in praise for evermore. Children, you too will fight bravely with him. And we know many of you will be martyred too. But Davidito will be the greatest martyr of all. Praise be to Grandpa, wise Grandpa, for choosing this special child as his son.'

My bottom lip stuck right out in temper.

I glared at Joy. I was furious with jealousy. How come he got to be the prince? I was going to die too, so why was he more glorious than me? And why did they have to make a book about him? I didn't know this little boy but I decided right there and then I did not like him.

I stared down at the book. To me it was just more evidence of the special attention this horrible boy was getting. Attention I wanted.

I was still sulking about it when the weekend came around. Unusually my father was home and we got to spend all day Sunday with him. As we sat on the end of my parents' bed I demanded to know why Davidito was so special.

'Because he is, Natacha,' said my father. 'Jesus sent him to Moses David. David is our King and Davidito is our Prince.

One day you will make me so proud when you bravely follow him into battle.'

'But why is there a book about him?' I demanded.

He looked a little perplexed and asked where I had seen it. I explained that Joy had shown it to us. 'It's not really a children's book. It's a guide for us grown-ups. I am frankly surprised Joy showed it to you. She shouldn't have.'

As he said all that he frowned, something that made me even more curious. 'Daddy, what are they doing in the pictures?'

He went quiet for a moment, then looked at me intently. 'They are just playing, Natacha. It's not how we play.' With that he started tickling me until I laughed and squealed at him to stop, all thoughts of the little boy now forgotten.

In truth my dad had been disturbed by the Davidito book. He felt that children should not be raised with a feeling of shame towards sex, but he found the pictures of naked women fondling a little boy quite unsettling and definitely not the type of 'play' he'd ever do with his own kids.

My parents had taken another book, called the *Little Girl Dream*, in much the same way. That book had a cover depicting a cartoon likeness of Berg and Maria in bed with a naked little girl. It was presented to members as 'spiritual guidance'.

But some members were beginning to feel more and more uncomfortable about the way other teachings were heading. New recruits had been expected to spend hours poring over the New Testament, the actual Bible. But as the years progressed they read the real Bible less and less. David Berg's writings had grown in importance and volume. So much material – books, Mo letters, videos and tapes – arrived at the communes that sometimes they barely had time to digest it before the next boxes of new material landed.

The Mo letters were unapologetic about this. 'And I want to frankly tell you,' he proclaimed, 'if there's a choice between your reading the Bible, I want to tell you, you had better read what God said today in preference to what he said 2,000 or 4,000 years ago!'

His followers bought this because, after all, in their eyes Father David/King David/David Moses – however they chose to refer to him – was undoubtedly God's true prophet.

Those who did question were labelled doubters and put under watch for suspected mind poisoning of other members, which created an environment of fear and paranoia.

During sharing sessions women were often asked to reveal if their husband was having doubts or struggling with 'demons'. They were told that revealing any doubts would help their partner to overcome them. This served to break down trust between couples and it's no surprise that many marriages broke up because of this.

Soon Mom was pregnant again. My little brother Vincent arrived screaming into the world in winter 1986.

I will never forget the moment I first laid eyes on his wrinkled pink face. He was adorable. I felt such a rush of love as I solemnly promised him that his big sister would always be there to look after him.

Chapter 5

Terror in the Shed

'Shut up, you wicked little beast.'

An uncle grabbed the back of Simon's T-shirt, yanking him up off the ground. Simon kicked out furiously with his legs and arms. I knew what they were going to do. Another uncle took a roll of masking tape and tore off a long strip. Simon screamed as he clenched his fists and began pummelling at his aggressor, who brushed his blows aside. Simon took his chance, biting milk teeth into fleshy forearm.

'You little shit. Hurry up, Matthew. The little bastard just bit me.'

'Yeah? He's a devil child all right,' said the second uncle, laughing. He stuck the masking tape over Simon's mouth, then added another two strips on top before patting it all down and standing back as if surveying his handiwork. Simon went completely quiet for a few seconds before making snuffled, panicked breaths through his nose. The uncle put him down and slapped him hard in the small of the back, causing his legs to buckle. 'Now get to class. Spare the rod, spoil the child. You will thank me for this when you grow up to be a better man. Praise the Lord.'

I was trying not to cry and they knew it; both of them were looking straight at me with a questioning expression. I pulled what I thought was a cute face. It worked – the second uncle ruffled my hair and walked on ahead. I could hear Simon whimpering through the tape. I took his hand and squeezed it tight.

Simon was considered a naughty child. He had tantrums where he threw himself on the floor and made his body go limp so no one could pick him up. He cried constantly for no reason. The adults didn't have any patience for it. Someone had the idea of taping his mouth up, and quickly that became the routine way of dealing with him. I heard my brother Matt say he wished Simon would just learn to stop crying so they wouldn't have to hurt him.

At lunchtime Simon yelled out loud as they yanked the duct tape off. The skin on his upper lip was red and broken. He refused to eat his rice and eggs and started to make a whiny sound. After five minutes of the noise, Aunty Joy was instructed to hold him down while a different uncle taped him up again. I don't know where his mother was or if she saw any of this happen.

The first time it happened I screamed with fear and got a big stinging slap around my face. I hated seeing pain inflicted on another child. For me, those hurting him were the naughty ones, not Simon. I tried to stay as close to him as I could because I knew it made him feel better.

A few days later I was just on my way to bed when I heard a loud commotion. Simon had fallen from a window and was lying on the ground. I wanted to check he was OK but a firm hand on my shoulder stopped me. All the children were ordered to our rooms and told to stay silent. Soon after I was told that his family had left.

There was only one main bathroom for children's use in Phuket, so several of us had to queue for the same single sink. We never jostled or fought openly because we knew that would get us into trouble. To the eyes of the various aunties and uncles who stood guard over us, we each waited patiently, politely and in silence. But in the secret world of children it was a different story. You'd inevitably hear hurtful names under someone's breath, or feel a sharp elbow in the ribs, a Chinese burn or a vicious nip by another kid who had perfected the art of hidden violence without an adult noticing. You had to take it without fuss because shouting out or complaining would surely end with a spanking.

Once a day children had to 'report' on each other when our teachers asked us to say out loud who had been naughty and why. The fear at reporting sessions was palpable because you never knew who would say what about you. Some kids blatantly made up lies about others, but stories were never challenged, just accepted as truth and the alleged perpetrator punished. Even if you knew the kid hadn't done anything you couldn't speak up and defend them because then you'd get a beating too. When another child was disciplined with the fly-swat, or as Simon was with the tape, we were forced to watch. All this was supposed to be for our spiritual benefit and to make us better Christians. But really all it did was turn us into nasty little snitches.

On this evening I had been at the back of the queue and was the last child to reach the sink. My roommates had all gone back into the dorm and were getting into bed. A few days earlier Aunty Joy had been replaced by a male teacher. His name was Uncle Clay. That wasn't his real name but his cult baptised name. Clay proudly explained it came from one of Grandpa's letters in which Grandpa explained that, to truly serve God, members had to be like clay on a potter's wheel – mouldable, willing to change and adapt to the moves of the spirit world.

I wept when Joy told us she was leaving. I loved her so much and I saw more of her than I did my own mother. She didn't hug us goodbye, she just told us one night at bedtime that Jesus was sending us a new teacher. In the morning she wasn't there. I ran around all the rooms in the house calling her name and looking for her, but I couldn't find her anywhere. I don't think I really accepted she was never coming back.

Clay was from the Philippines, short and plump with greasy black hair, a potbelly and acne-cratered skin. His breath was rank and sometimes he spat when he talked. It made me feel ill just to look at him. Within the Family hierarchy looking after children or cooking was considered a lowly role. Witnessing, fundraising and public relations were the cushy 'status' jobs all the adults wanted. Clay was openly bitter and resentful at his lowly position.

I was brushing my teeth when he walked in. He had known I was alone. He shut the door and came and stood right behind me – too close – towering over me with his adult presence. He was naked bar a small towel around his waist. It barely covered his bulging stomach. I could smell his unwashed body.

'Have you had a shower, Natacha?' he asked in a creepy voice.

I spat out the toothpaste before I choked on it. 'Yes, Uncle Clay,' I answered politely as I tried to dart past him.

He grabbed me by the arm. 'You need another one.'

He lifted my nightie over my head, folded it neatly and placed it on the towel rack. Then he led me to the shower, roughly pushed me in and turned it on. He removed his towel. As he turned to put it on the rack I shrank at the thick black hair that covered his shoulders. I dared not move. He got in with me. Then he took my hand and placed it on his penis. I froze. I had a sense this was wrong, very wrong. He put his hand over mine and slid it up and down over him. I screwed my eyes tightly shut as he began praising God over and over again. 'Hallelujah, praise the Lord, hallelujah!'

When it was finished he washed himself thoroughly while I stood there numbly. Then he took the soap and lathered me with intrusive hands. I shifted and tried to wriggle away but he just laughed. His acne-pocked face broke into a toothy smile and I noticed his skin seemed to shine with grease. As he rubbed me with a flannel he told me I had been a very good girl. He didn't need to ask me not to tell anyone.

He dried me methodically with the towel. He took a long time, almost deliberately as if to remind me how powerful and in control he was. Then he placed my nightie back over my head before patting me on the bottom and ordering me to get myself to bed. Without a word I did as he asked, climbing silently into my bunk. The other children were all asleep. I was too shocked to cry. Despite the wash I felt dirty and I could still smell him on my hands. I lay there staring at the dark wall for a long time.

It happened again about a week later. During nap time I felt a hand touch my stomach. I tensed, not sure what to expect. The hand slid into my pants. I felt like I needed to vomit but I held still, too scared to be spanked if I moved. His fingers moved, pawing at me. I kept my eyes firmly shut.

I could smell his rotten breath as he moaned: 'Thank you, Jesus, oh God, hallelujah,' over and over. His fingers moved harder until the friction began to hurt. He continued to praise God but his breathing became heavier. A few minutes later I felt a shudder of movement as he gave one big groan. I heard him pick up the bottle of diluted Dettol that was on his bedside table. As he sprayed his hands with it the smell floated towards me. I desperately tried to hold back the waves of nausea that rose in my throat. I still didn't open my eyes.

The following day I was able to snatch a few minutes alone with my mother. During break time she was sitting in the garden feeding one of the babies. She had been given a job, or 'ministry' as it was termed, in the nursery. I ran over to her and burst into tears. She hugged me and whispered: 'Natacha, why do you cry? What's wrong, *ma chérie*?'

I pressed my face against hers, comforted by the scent of her long blonde hair. I wanted so badly to communicate to her what had happened. But at four years old I couldn't find the language or words to describe it. I so badly wanted her maternal instinct to understand, to look at me and somehow *know*.

Instead she wiped my tears and smiled: 'Ah, *chérie*. Get the victory. Shall we pray together and ask Jesus to make it better for you?'

I hated that phrase. If we fell over and grazed a knee we were not comforted but urged to 'get the victory'. If we struggled with memorising our Bibles we were told to 'get the victory'. It never made anything better.

So on the day I woke up with a fever I didn't expect much sympathy from the grown-ups. All night I had shivered and sweated, freezing cold one minute and boiling hot the next. I could barely touch my cereal at breakfast. Aunty Salome, who was supervising, put her hand to my forehead and frowned. 'You *are* very hot, aren't you?'

I looked at her expectantly, half hoping she'd tell me to go back to bed. But she didn't and instead I was ordered to go straight to class. Sitting at my desk was agony. I was beginning to feel delirious, and when I was asked a question I could barely register the words I was hearing. I failed to answer correctly and was told to hold my hands out while they were rapped with a ruler for lack of concentration. My shirt was soaked with sweat, which made me feel cold and clammy.

No one considered taking me to a doctor because Grandpa said faith alone would heal illness. Going to a doctor showed a lack of trust in God and his power to heal. The only exceptions were when someone's life was clearly at risk or for mothers-to-be, who were allowed to give birth in a hospital if they wished. I knew I had been born in a run-down local hospital because my dad had told me the story. He proudly told me he had insisted on it because he wanted to be sure his precious little girl was born safely, but he also said system people were so silly because they took pills when they had something as basic as a headache. They didn't know the devil made the pills and used it to control their minds. He told me when he was younger and before he joined the group, he too had been controlled this way, so he knew from personal experience how evil medicine could be.

Personal computers, which were just beginning to enter the mainstream, were viewed with equal suspicion. In a Mo letter Grandpa had told us that using one would also result in the Antichrist putting a chip in your head to control you. In Word Time we read a storybook about a man this actually happened to. The devil made him do all sorts of bad things. In the end he had to have lots of sex with different women to get cured. One lady was able to take the chip out during a love-up session when he was distracted. Afterwards he was really grateful to her and fell in love with her.

Even the songs churned out by cult production teams added to the fear of outside control. There was one called 'Cathy Don't Go (to the Supermarket Today)'. The song was about a woman called Cathy who wanted to buy discounted bags of rice at the supermarket. The chorus, which had sinister vibrating guitar sounds, warned her not to go because a strange man would use the till's scanning machine to put a chip into her hand so he could control and capture her.

By mid-afternoon I was seriously ill and unable to stand. Eventually I was carried to my room by an uncle and placed on the bed. I was left alone for several hours, crying for my mother and drifting in and out of sleep, when I became aware of Clay and two other adults standing over me. 'She's probably contagious. We need to be careful or they will all get it.'

Clay put his hand on my forehead and stroked my cheek. The next thing I was aware of was him lifting me up and carrying me out the back door of the house. Another uncle walked behind him carrying food supplies and bottles of water. Behind the house there was a wooden shed with a small double bed, which I knew was used by visiting Shepherds for sharing because my brothers had seen people having sex in there. The other uncle unlatched the door as Clay carried me inside and placed me on the bed. The room smelt like the bedrooms did during the grown-ups' love-up times – a mixture of sweat and disinfectant. It was also so hot it was like being in a greenhouse. I could barely breathe.

The uncle turned to Clay. 'She doesn't look good. Should I go find Patience?'

I tried to move and nod my head yes. Clay saw me and told me to lie still. 'No, she'll be good,' he replied. 'The important thing is she doesn't infect the other kids. I'll stay with her until the fever breaks.'

'You're a good man, Clay,' said the uncle, patting him on the back before leaving me to Clay's mercy.

I was almost asleep when I became aware of Clay rubbing his hand up and down my leg. I tried to clamp my knees together. He forced them apart and continued.

I was kept in the shed with just Clay for company, drifting in and out of consciousness. I don't know how long I was there, but it seemed endless. At times Clay did behave like a care giver, urging me to eat oatmeal as he held out a spoon. I tried to swallow but I was too weak to control my bodily functions and couldn't even lift my head off the pillow or open my mouth. Occasionally he spoke soothing words of comfort, telling me I would feel better soon. But mostly he used me to pleasure himself, taking full advantage of a sick four-year-old child for his own twisted perversions.

I believe my mind is unable to deal with the horror and has blocked out some of the worst of what happened. I couldn't say just how far the abuse went or whether Clay had full sex with me. It is a dark place I do not want to return to. But the sensory images are always with me, playing out in nightmarish flashbacks: his unwashed skin, hairy armpits and sweat dripping on my face as he leaned over me, the smell of dettol, his fingernails grabbing at my skin and his thick Filipino accent as he gave thanks to the Lord for delivering me to him. I have visions of him rubbing my body up and down over himself and arched against me, rocking.

Whenever I came round I cried and cried for my mother, but I am certain she had no idea how ill I was or where I had been taken, or she would have come for me. I suppose it is possible that she visited while I was asleep or delirious and thought I was being looked after. She would never have imagined what Clay was doing to me in the darkness of that shed; that a man she trusted to take care of her child had committed the very worst of sins.

She had no idea that her little girl would never be the same again.

Chapter 6

Candles and Confessions

In the days and weeks that followed I became even more fidgety, constantly scratching myself or twitching my legs. I had trouble sleeping, not least because Clay was so often in the room at night with us. I was constantly on edge, wondering if and when he might hurt me again.

My dad was still away most of the time and I saw less and less of my mom and Leah. I still missed Joy and began to lose interest in lessons. At least Joy tried to make them fun. Clay had zero interest in teaching kids and didn't care if we understood anything or not. I was so scared of him now that even the sound of his voice made my hands start to tremble and my legs involuntarily go into spasm.

I didn't have the words to articulate to anyone what had happened to me. I didn't even know for sure it was wrong. I only knew I had hated it, it hurt me and that it made me feel dirty. Worse, I had a strong sense that it was definitely something I would be in big trouble for if I ever told.

So I kept quiet.

Each morning when I woke up my first action was to look over to the single bed in our room and see if he was in it. If he was I stayed silent and still as a church mouse. If the bed was empty I could relax a little and chat to my friends.

One morning, a little after dawn, I got a surprise.

Someone switched the light on. 'Up time, children. We are going out to sing the praises of the Lord.'

It was my mother! Rarely did she come into our room. I was delighted. 'Mommy! Good morning.'

'And good morning to you, my darling. Good morning to all you lovely children. Good morning, Jesus. Good morning, love. Good morning, good morning, good morning.'

She was laughing and doing little twirls around the room. We were delighted. 'More. More, Mommy, please.' She beamed her radiant smile towards me and winked. 'Okay, Natacha, just for you.'

Then she rose up and up, arching her feet until she was standing on the very tops of her tiptoes, her arms up high above her head in a perfect arc.

'Wow,' said one of the other girls.

I beamed with pride. To me, my mommy was one of the most beautiful ladies in the world and I was intensely proud of her past as a ballerina. This was something I regularly boasted about to the other girls. As they all gawped in wonder at her moves I thought I might burst with pride. At that precise moment I don't think I could have loved her more.

She was as giddy and excited as a little girl herself as she hurried us along to get up and ready. We were going out into the city to take the love of Jesus to the needy, she explained to us. And this meant another bonus – we got to dress up.

Material possessions, including clothes, were generally frowned upon. That was convenient because we didn't have enough money to buy new clothes anyway. The women wore long skirts and T-shirts (no bra or underwear), men tended to wear shorts or jeans with a T-shirt, and we kids wore whatever could be reused, handed down or had been donated by well-wishers. I had only two sets of clothes for everyday use – a frayed pair of old jeans that had been my brother's, some shorts and two tops. But when we were sent out witnessing, like we were today, we got dressed in our special clothes. Cute white kids performing songs and dances in frilly dresses, ankle socks and bonnets pretty much guaranteed bigger donations.

My best witnessing dress was made of pale yellow satin with a ruffled skirt and a matching hat. I hated the sensation of it on my head, especially in the boiling hot sun. It made my head itch. But I loved the dress and the lacy hemline on the skirt.

We ate breakfast – blackened, mushy bananas that had been sitting out for too long. Then we were ordered into the battered commune minivan. The van rarely got used because petrol was considered a luxury and a system thing. It was usually left parked out on the driveway in the sun. As we got in I was hit by a wave of intense sauna-like heat that made it hard to breathe. One little girl started to cry and Clay tried to calm her down by shouting at her. I shrank back into my seat. Sitting next to Clay was Ezekiel. I glared at his back, hoping a thunderbolt would follow. I hated his guts.

Then an unexpected visitor got in the front seat. My dad.

He turned to face us with a grin. 'Well, *bonjour*. I got back home late last night so I decided to come with you all today. I hope that is OK with everyone?'

The men nodded deferentially. My dad was a leader so of course it had to be OK.

We drove for about three hours. The sun was reaching its midday peak by the time we found a parking spot on the edge of the city. We could never afford to pay for car parks so we often drove around a city for ages, trying to find a free spot. I don't know which city we went to because no one bothered to tell us. It didn't really matter anyway. All of the places we visited for witnessing were system cities with system names. They were inhabited by systemite people who in our eyes were foolish and lost. Our job was to warn them of the End Time and urge them to save their souls by joining us or, better still, giving us some money. We usually formed into little groups of two adults and a couple of kids before splitting up and taking different sections of a neighbourhood. Some went into shops, other knocked on doors of houses. The day was turning out better than I had hoped when my father picked me up and whispered that he, Mom and I were going to form our own little group for the day. 'And we are going to come back with the most money, aren't we, Natacha? Do you think you can do that? Can you help Mommy and Daddy do this?'

I was grinning my face off, too happy to speak.

Three hours of door knocking later and the novelty factor of spending time with my parents had well and truly worn off. We were walking around tree-lined streets with rows of green-roofed villas set behind lush gardens. Dogs barked and voices rang out from behind the walls. I was hungry, dehydrated and exhausted. Hours of selling the End Time in the middle of a tropical afternoon began to play with my mind, and I was half expecting a red demon with horns and a tail to come rushing out and eat me. My satin dress was so hot and stifling, I longed to tear it off and go naked –

anything to feel cooler for even a second. I kept pulling my hat off but my mother kept putting it back on my head, telling me it looked nice. She may have been right about the hat but my scowl certainly wasn't sweet.

At each house my dad did the knocking and the talking while my mom stood there beaming, either holding onto my hand or carrying me so the occupants could get a better look. Old ladies cooed over me and little children laughed and pointed. I was like an animal in a zoo. Women insisted on touching my strawberry-blonde locks to see if they were real; they stroked my cheeks and kissed my head. I hated it. I hated being touched at the best of times, but the constant physical attention by systemites, whom I knew to be bad people, was completely traumatic.

I was really struggling not to cry by this point. Fortunately for me a French woman lived in the next house we knocked at. She recognised my parents' accents and started talking to them in French. They were delighted and began jabbering back. The woman was pleased but a little bemused to find two of her countrymen selling Christian literature in a Buddhist country and was curious to find out more. Where had they come from? How long had they been here? She invited us in. I could have wept with joy when we walked into her hallway with its cool marble floor. She ushered us into the living room. I had never seen anything so beautiful in all my life.

There was a big sofa with fat velvet cushions, long flowery curtains and bookshelves lined with hundreds and hundreds of pretty candles in all sorts of different colours and patterns. My eyes roamed wildly, trying to take it all in. She saw me and smiled. 'I see you like the candles? I make them. That's my hobby.'

The house was so clean and tidy, nothing like the overcrowded, worn-out living spaces in the commune. I wanted to touch everything.

The lady had a son a couple of years older than me. While she sat and talked to my parents she instructed her son to take me into his bedroom and show me some of his toys. He opened a huge box stuffed full of teddy bears, cars and figurines. He was generous, letting me touch any toy I liked. At one point the lady came up to check on us and brought us an ice lolly each. I began to think this place might even be heaven.

All too soon I heard Mom shouting up the stairs. 'Natacha, *ma chérie*, we must leave now. Say thank you to the lady.'

I didn't move. I think I hoped if I said nothing they might forget I was there or go without me. Not to be. A few minutes later my father came bounding up, looking cross. He reached down to pick me up. I clung onto a small fluffy bear that I had fallen in love with. The little boy looked at me, then at the bear, then back at me.

'She can keep it,' he said to my dad firmly.

'No, she cannot,' said my dad, more for my benefit than the little boy's.

'It's OK,' the boy replied. 'I have lots of them and I think she really likes him.'

My father didn't reply. Instead he grabbed the bear out of my vice-like grip and put it down on the bed. '*No*.'

We were barely a few feet away from the gate when I started to yell – great big gulping sobs of anger and hurt. By the time we caught up with the other teams I was sobbing so much my breathing was erratic. My parents studiously ignored me, presumably thinking I'd stop when I got bored.

Usually my occasional temper tantrums didn't last long, but this time I just couldn't stop crying.

Everyone was hungry, having not eaten all day. The mission now was to find a restaurant that was willing to feed us for free. We hadn't raised enough to be able to buy dinner for the ten adults and children that formed our total party. As we paced a nearby market, the adults asking stallholders to donate some food, my father had to tow me behind him, my feet dragging in the dust, snot dribbling down my filthy cheeks. I looked like a sad ragamuffin clown, such a pathetic sight that eventually a food vendor took pity.

'Little girl is sad. Poor girl. Come inside,' she said, ushering us towards the wooden bench seats outside her little restaurant.

She bent down so she was at my height and looked at me with kindly brown eyes. 'No cry, little girl. Be happy. Always be happy.'

I know she was trying to be nice but her kindness just made it worse. I paused for a split second before letting out another series of great gasping sobs.

I don't think I was crying because my father wouldn't let me keep the little boy's teddy bear. I was crying for the life I had glimpsed. I was crying for the kindly candle-maker and her neat house. I was crying for a normal family like theirs.

However, compared to my brother Vincent I was a blissfully happy child. From the day he was born Vincent was different. He was sensitive, quiet, teary and thoughtful. He was also always in trouble.

Within The Family, parenting was a shared responsibility. If an adult saw you do something wrong they didn't have to tell your parents about it, they just went ahead and sorted you out themselves. For the aunts and uncles, themselves often hungry, tired and under stress, the burden of dealing with other people's children was often a pure annoyance. Of course there were exceptions like Joy who genuinely loved kids, but most adults I came across, even those with their own children, seemed to treat us as an irritation at best, devil spawn at worst. And Vincent had an innate ability to bring out the worst in them.

When he was 11 months old he was caught sucking the sugar coating off a packet of tablets. He didn't know what they were and, of course, if he'd eaten them it could have been dangerous. They shouldn't even have been left within a small child's reach. But fortunately he licked them and then put them back in the packet after reaching the bitter centre. Ezekiel found him. He picked him up by his skinny little arms and screamed that he was going to thrash him. Vincent yelled at the top of his lungs, and my eldest brother, Joe, ran in. When he saw what was happening he begged Ezekiel not to hurt little Vincent but to thrash him instead. The monster took him outside into the garden and beat him black and blue with a plank.

Getting hit – be it with fists, fly-swats, poles and planks – was all part of the cult children's daily routine. On one occasion an uncle, I don't know who because they were too scared to say, threw all of my brothers into an empty bathtub naked and hit them with a wooden paddle as they dived under each other to shield themselves from the blows.

I don't think my parents ever really knew just how much the other adults meted out violence to their children. Dad was so rarely there and my mother didn't seem to notice how unhappy we were. Perhaps that's because in the few moments of quality time we did get to spend with her, we were so delighted by it we never stopped smiling.

The closest they got to understanding came about four months after Clay had abused me in the shed. One of the bigger girls told me in hushed tones that two senior Shepherds were here and they wanted to see each kid individually. I didn't believe her until we were all called into the dining hall and told to sit in silence and wait our turns. We were not given the chance to ask what was going on and were expressly forbidden from talking to each other. When it was my turn to go in the room I was shaking with nerves. Why would Shepherds want to talk to me? Had I done something bad?

I walked into the room where an aunty and uncle I didn't know were sitting on two chairs with another facing them. They gestured me to sit down.

'Now, Natacha,' said the uncle, 'I am going to ask you a question and I want you to tell me the truth. Don't be frightened.'

I nodded.

'Has anyone ever touched you? Touched you in a bad way?'

My legs started to shake and my mouth went dry. I wanted to scratch an itch on my face. I could have told them the truth about Clay but my survival instinct kicked in. Instinctively I knew the answer they wanted.

I looked them straight in the eye and said no. They asked me a few more questions, and then told me I was a good girl and I could go now.

The next morning after breakfast the children were told to stay behind because the grown-ups had something important to say to us. Salome spoke. In low calm tones she asked us if we loved The Family.

'Yes,' we trilled in unison.

'And are you grateful for your loving family?' she asked. Yes again.

'And are you aware that God loves you? Are you aware that the devil wants to take you as his own? Are you aware that unless we love and appreciate our family we will fall into the path of evil?'

On and on she went as we repeated yes to every question.

Finally came her point. 'Are you aware that God tested you yesterday by sending some messengers to ask you questions?'

As we nodded she raised her eyebrows. 'So you are aware of this? I know some of you gave godly answers. But how was it one wicked child gave an answer formed by the devil himself?'

At that she flew across the room and grabbed a terrified girl called Samantha. She was older than me, about 13. It seems Samantha had told the Shepherds that Uncle Ezekiel had made her do things to him.

I knew I had made the right choice about staying quiet when Salome forced a bar of soap into Samantha's mouth, barking at her to eat it to wash away her lies and sinful nature. All of us, from toddlers to teens, stood watching, motionless and powerless.

After it was over Samantha was allowed a glass of water and was shoved back into her chair. She was ordered to remain silent for the next week. Any child caught talking to her would get the same punishment. Then we were sent back to class. No one dared even look at poor Samantha.

When she came back into class later she had a handwritten cardboard sign tied around her neck with string, which read: *I am on silence restriction for telling lies. Please do not speak to me*. Her eyes were red and puffy as she shuffled shamefacedly into her seat.

My father had missed this whole debacle. As usual he was in Bangkok when the Shepherds had visited. But he knew that similar investigations were happening in all communes in response to allegations of abuse within The Family, the story making it into the international media. In a bid to protect the group's reputation and make it look like they were doing something, David Berg had ordered all communes to talk to the children and find out their stories.

I badly wanted to tell an adult about my experiences with Clay but I was also very confused. No one had ever explained to me that things like that were wrong. It was only the sick feeling in my stomach that made me think there was something bad about it.

I had been brought up to fear and respect adults, and to never question their decisions. That made me think that what Clay did was probably normal or something that every other adult did to children.

Ezekiel soon disappeared, and not long after that Clay vanished too. No one told me why. Not knowing if he was coming back or not made me worry even more.

My trauma was showing in other ways, had anyone bothered to look hard enough. I was becoming severely anxious at any slight change to routine. At night I still couldn't sleep, often waking up crying.

One night as I climbed into my bed I felt someone looking at me. Startled, I turned, fearing Clay had returned. Instead I saw a little girl in a long white dress staring straight at me. She didn't smile but something about her presence calmed me.

Over the next few days I saw her everywhere, walking in front of me to class and standing next to me as I ate.

I like to believe she was my guardian angel.

Chapter 7

Torn Apart

The Children of God might have renamed themselves The Family in a bid to make some kind of point about communal values, but when I was seven we came to learn just how little families like ours really meant to them.

It was early morning, when the tropical heat was at its most bearable. Birds sang their wake-up calls, swooping onto the flame of the forest tree with twigs in their mouths ready for nest building. A red-and-yellow butterfly fluttered down and paused on my hand before flying away. I watched it go before turning back to the confusing scene on the driveway.

An uncle was loading Leah and Thérèse's scarce possessions into the minivan. My mother and Leah were standing next to it, hugging each other. I didn't really understand what was going on but I had a sense it was very bad, and because Mom and Leah cried it was only natural I did too.

My brothers hung near them, trying to cling to Leah's legs. With a determined look on his face Marc climbed into the van, picked up the bags and started to carry them back towards the house. The uncle grabbed them and put them back into the van.

'No, no, no.' Marc flung himself at Leah from behind, gripping onto her as if his life depended on it. My mother walked behind, gently trying to prise him away, but he screamed and clung even tighter.

My parents had been ordered to a new commune in Bangkok; Leah and Thérèse had been ordered to a different city. Leah was highly valued as a flirty fisher and she was still technically single because, although in a committed relationship with my father, she wasn't married to him. In short, her assets were too useful for her to be allowed to stay in the threesome any longer.

The senior Shepherds who made the decision had sprung the news on us while my father was away on a mission, denying him the chance to say goodbye to his long-term lover and their daughter. As the minivan prepared to drive away with my beloved baby sister in it, I pressed my face against the window and blew a kiss to Thérèse, who had tears rolling down her tiny cheeks. She was just six. I was seven. As I waved goodbye I could never have imagined that it would be a decade before I saw her again.

We weren't the only family to be broken up in such a brutal way. Siblings were sent away, married people separated, older children ripped from their parents – all on the whims of the leadership. I had heard my older brothers talking about how the mother of a friend of theirs had left The Family by running away in the middle of the night. She came back with some men a few weeks later to try to kidnap her son, but the Shepherds had been expecting her to try it and had already sent him to another country so she couldn't find him.

My dad was still a Regional Shepherd but was beginning to see his authority wane. David Berg was paranoid about anyone becoming too powerful or challenging his dominance. As such he created a management ethos based on game playing, backstabbing and blame. Even at local leadership level it was impossible to get too comfortable in your role because it seemed that however hard you worked or how competent you were it was never quite enough. Dad had been a Shepherd for over ten years now, and some may have felt that was too long.

The night after Leah and Thérèse left was horrible. My mom looked pale and in pain, the boys wouldn't stop crying and I was completely confused, still half expecting them to come back in through the door. Then we had the added turmoil of knowing that we were also on the move at the crack of dawn. Mom tried to be positive about it, saying that as Dad was in Bangkok so often anyway it was a very good thing because we could see much more of him.

I was sad to leave some of my friends but I was pleased to see the back of that place.

By 7 a.m. we were on the road, a ragtag family in a battered minibus, a few bundles of clothes our only possessions. The roads were winding and rough, which made me feel so ill we had to stop the car twice for me to vomit by the side of the road.

As we reached the outskirts of Bangkok I thought we had driven into hell itself. It was a terrifyingly teeming, bustling, overwhelming city that made Phuket look like a tiny village. I had never seen so much traffic or heard so much awful noise. At the traffic lights a man in uniform banged on the window. I saw his uniform and screamed: 'Antichrist!'

'It's OK, *ma chérie*. He's just a system policeman. He was only helping us through the traffic,' explained my mother.

Her words did nothing to help me understand. I'd always been told the systemites in uniform *were* the Antichrist's followers and were the most dangerous of all. When the End Time came they were the very people who would want to kill us. So why was it that whenever we went outside my parents spoke to them?

Once we'd traversed the city centre we reached a suburb on the far side. We turned off down a dusty unmade road, surrounded by boggy fields mostly, with a few half-constructed villas along the side. After a kilometre or so we arrived in front of a house with a large red metal gate and a high concrete wall with broken splinters of glass sticking out the top. We beeped the horn and the gate swung open to reveal our new home, a two-storey concrete building with a cluster of smaller one-storey buildings set around a central courtyard. I was disappointed to see there was no beautiful flame of the forest tree here. There was hardly any garden at all, just a few bedraggled shrubs here and there. Virtually all the space had been given over to the buildings.

We walked into a mess hall where over 150 people were eating lunch in silence. They all turned to stare at us. No one got up to say hello. I started to cry, grabbing at my mother's skirt. 'Mommy, I want to go back home.'

She bent down to reassure me just as a strange uncle walked up and gave us instructions about where we would sleep. My mom didn't even have time to hug me before he announced her 'mission' was as usual to work in the nursery looking after the babies. He picked up her little bag and started walking through the hall, waiting for her to follow. When she hesitated he snapped rudely at her: 'Come on then, I haven't got all day.' The pair disappeared out of view.

My brothers and I stood there waiting uncertainly for another ten minutes. The older boys stood with ramrod-straight backs, outwardly calm but watchful and aware. I got the impression they were as worried as I was but that they were trying to look strong for Vincent and me. I followed their lead by holding onto Vincent's hand, hoping it would make him feel better.

The uncle came back. My eldest brother, Joe, found his voice, politely asking: 'Excuse me, Uncle, but please can you tell me where my father is? Is he here?'

'Yes,' replied the man. 'He's busy with his work in the Shepherd's offices. You will see him later. Don't bother him now.'

He gestured for us to pick up our bags and follow him. As we walked he explained that all children slept in age-related dormitories. The dorms were as follows: YCs (younger children), MCs (middle children), OCs (older children), JETTs (Jesus End Time teens), JTs (junior teens) and STs (senior teens).

I was put in the MCs and Vincent the YCs. 'I want to stay with Tacha,' he pleaded to the uncle but the man barely even glanced down at him before handing him over to the aunty who ran his dorm.

The MC dorm was crammed with over a dozen double and triple bunks, with extra trundle beds on wheels underneath the bunks. The uncle pointed to a bottom bunk with a thin foam mattress. On one wall there was a large freestanding cupboard with several drawers. He picked out a tiny drawer in the middle where I was instructed to store my spare set of clothes.

The rest of the day passed in a haze of anxiety. As I climbed onto my new bed no one spoke to me, although several children stared at me blankly. I felt wretched, wishing so badly my mom would come and cuddle me. I thought about Leah and Thérèse. With the optimistic logic of a child, a little bit of me had hoped they might be waiting for us in Bangkok. With the final realisation they weren't, I cried myself quietly to sleep.

I was woken at 6 a.m. by a completely naked aunty ordering us into the bathroom with her. The bathroom was large, with a basic Asian style shower – an oil drum full of water in the corner, a plastic bucket and a jug to splash water over ourselves. The other kids still ignored me. They had hollow, weird eyes that made me feel creepy. I was too scared to say anything to them. After the shower we all dressed in silence and marched single file into the mess hall for breakfast.

After breakfast my schooling regime was explained to me. The routine here was much more regimented than it had been in Phuket. The day was a constant round of Word Time (studying Grandpa's teachings), followed by Memorising (memorising Grandpa's teachings), Jesus Job Time (housework such as scrubbing floors or washing dishes), School Work (which wasn't academic but involved more of Grandpa's teachings), preparing for the End Time and Quiet Time (forced nap time).

At all times children were forbidden to talk without permission. That was also the rule in Phuket but even the likes of Clay and Ezekiel, as terrible as they were, didn't usually bother to enforce it. Here was different: I found to my cost that even a stolen whisper to my brother in the mess hall resulted in being sent 'to the wall', where you had to stand with your nose to the wall for up to an hour without moving. The first time it happened to me I got horrible cramps in my back and leg but when I moved I got a spank.

A few days after we moved in, the home began its annual 'fast'. All communes in The Family fasted for three days leading up to Berg's birthday, which was a day of ecstatic celebration for his followers. The entire house fell into what felt like a state of mourning. All daily operations, fundraising and events were cancelled. A few adults took care of the children and cooking in rotating shifts while the others spent 72 hours in prayer vigils, inspiration time and reading dozens of long letters from Grandpa. During the fast they were allowed to eat only liquid foods. I remember the large bowls of soup and a gooey pale orange mix of papaya blended with yogurt that sat on the counters in the dining room as the adults filed by us in complete silence, almost as if in a trance. Pregnant women and children were exempt from fasting, although we little ones had to spent extra time reading Grandpa's letters and praying. Every evening the home would gather together for inspiration time, which was twice as long as normal. To me it seemed like endlessly dull hours of singing with the incants of praying in tongues floating through the house. It only served to add to my unhappiness at being there.

Within a couple of weeks I had begun to make friends – a boy called Noah and two sisters, Faith and Mary. Our friendship didn't amount to much more than exchanging smiles or silently taking a place next to theirs in the classroom. But just being able to sit next to a child I knew wasn't hostile helped me feel more settled. After a few weeks of being there I was beginning to sleep more easily. My all-pervading of fear of Clay was fading. My new bed was far from cosy but I took a certain reassurance in sharing the room with so many kids. That night I climbed in and fell straight to sleep.

'Inspection time, MCs,' the voice startled me awake. I could make out the silhouettes of an aunty and uncle who had come into our room. Disoriented, I thought for a minute they meant a tidy bunk inspection, and I was very confused as to why this was happening in the middle of the night instead of before breakfast like usual. I had clambered halfway out of my bed before it dawned on me I was the only one doing so. Two boys in the bed opposite had rolled over onto their fronts, faces buried in the pillow. My first thought was that they were going to be in trouble for ignoring the inspection. But then the aunty leaned over one of them and pulled down his pyjama bottoms as the uncle shone a torch. She took something and put it in his bottom. She pulled his pyjamas back up and moved to the kid above. I stared wordlessly as they moved methodically from child to child, repeating the process. No one was crying. As they reached my bed memories of Clay flooded back and I pulled the sheet up to my chin, shaking my head. The aunty looked surprised and turned to the uncle. He smiled. 'She's the new kid. Patience's daughter. They probably didn't have good cures in their old house.'

'Ah, got you,' said the aunty. She looked at me kindly. 'What's your name?'

'Natacha.'

'Hi, Natacha, I'm Aunty Rose. This is Uncle Zac. There's no need to be scared, sweetie. We've come to give you all some medicines. You need them so you don't get sick.'

'I'm not sick.'

'I know you're not. Not yet anyway. But if you don't take the medicine you might be. It's good for you.'

'Why?' I was surprised at my own boldness.

'OK, honey, have you heard of worms? Do you know what worms do?'

'Yes, they live in the ground.'

'They do. Some of them. But some of them live inside little children. They live in children's tummies and they grow bigger and bigger and bigger until they give you a nasty tummy ache. I want to give you some medicine to stop the worms getting inside your tummy. It's a lovely God-given natural cure to keep the nasty worms away. Can I do that?'

Still staring mistrustfully, I nodded silently.

'OK. I promise it won't hurt. Turn over, sweetie.'

With that she placed a large garlic clove inside my bottom.

She lied. I was so uncomfortable I couldn't get back to sleep afterwards. Nor did it do anything to prevent worms. Loads of the kids had them.

Chapter 8

Ruled by Fear

'Doe, a deer, a female deer. Ray, a drop of golden sun. Me, a name, I call myself. Far, a long long way to run.'

I sat cross-legged on the floor, gleefully singing at the top of my voice. Everyone was smiling and singing along with pure gusto. It was movie night and every occupant in the Bangkok commune we now called home was crammed into the dining hall to watch *The Sound of Music*. Movie night was our weekly treat. Talking was allowed, you got to sit with your family and everyone seemed to lighten up and be in a good mood. It was the highlight of my week and I loved it. If you'd been naughty you were not allowed to go. As a motivation to be good it was so effective, I would have done almost anything to be there. *The Sound of Music* was my favourite film in the whole world. I knew every line, every lyric. That's because we watched it almost every movie night.

The Shepherds controlled which films were suitable for us to watch, based on their orders from HQ. Films had to be moral, suitable for children and with a Christian message. That limited the choice somewhat, as did the fact we didn't have money to rent or buy alternative films. The only other movies I remember watching were *Jesus of Nazareth* and *Heidi*.

As we lined up to enter the living room, a Home Shepherd who was guarding the door had told us that only those who spoke in tongues would be allowed into the room to watch the movie. The door policy was usually either the tongues test or having to quote a verse from the Bible. Some of the kids made a real meal of it, throwing their hands up in the air theatrically to try to impress the adults with their spiritual talents.

One of the boys from the JETTs group went into show-off mode. With his eyes squeezed shut he scrunched his face and began shouting out in what we were told was the language of angels. 'Sheeba dee ba dee ba deee. Hambala abahala eba.' I watched him with disgust, appalled by what, to me, was such an obviously phoney display of spirituality. When it came to my turn I just clammed up. I always felt self-consciously stupid whenever I had to say anything in tongues. I think I knew even then the whole thing was ridiculous. But my reticence caused me to miss the first fifteen minutes of the movie because he wouldn't let me in until I got it right.

Once inside and when the film started, there was still no guarantee you'd get to watch it. At regular intervals it was paused for a moral teaching and group discussion. Sometimes it took over three hours to reach the closing credits. But I didn't care. Movie night was the most fun we ever had. And most importantly of all, I got to hang out with my mom and dad.

Our new routine was so strict that my parents were increasingly isolated from us, as were we siblings from each other.

At mealtimes we had to walk in single file and sit at communal tables with our age groups. Seeing my mother across the hall feeding a baby in a high chair was like a stab in the heart. My brothers and I had worked out a way of communicating through secret winks; getting an 'Are you OK?' wink from them cheered me up enormously.

Matt in particular looked exhausted, with big dark rings under his eyes. He'd been put on the 'early birds' programme, which meant getting up an hour before the other kids for extra study and prayer time.

The only quality time I got to spend with my family members was for a few hours on a Sunday, designated Family Time, when we were free to do whatever we wanted. Usually my brothers and I would pile into our parents' bedroom, sit on the bed and talk, talk, talk – telling my parents all about what we had learned that week. Sometimes we played marbles, but given how tiny their room was we always ended up losing the balls under the bed, spending more time crawling under it to get them than we did playing.

My brothers and I were so desperate for their attention we all jabbered at once, trying to be the cutest, the funniest or the sweetest child. The competition was intense and the time so short that it was impossible to tell them the bad things – the beatings, the bed-wetting and the horrible children who picked on me. Family Time was always over too quickly. I tried so hard to be brave and not to let them see me cry when it was time to go back to the dorm. It wasn't lost on us that Mom and Dad also battled hard to do the same as they kissed us goodbye.

There was a moment of family joy, though, with the birth of my brother Guy. I had been secretly hoping for another girl.

I still badly missed Thérèse, but when Guy arrived, all pink and cute just like Vincent had been, I fell instantly in love with him. He was in the nursery with Mom so she was able to breastfeed him herself (as she had all of us), but she certainly wasn't able to focus entirely on her newborn. New mothers were expected to share their milk and breastfeed other babies whose mothers were away FF'ing or fundraising.

Every day in the Bangkok house seemed to bring a set of strange new rules or procedures. Survival depended on adapting quickly. For example, using more than two pieces of toilet paper for a wee or three for a bowel movement got you a hard spank for being wasteful. The rationale was that we didn't have money to spare and God expected us to be thankful for the gifts we had; therefore over-using a roll of toilet paper was deemed a very unspiritual and selfish thing to do. To ensure we got the point we had to go with the door open while an adult hovered over us. It was so humiliating. Even getting permission to use the toilet in the first place was a minefield. Children weren't allowed to talk until spoken to so you couldn't just ask outright. I was told to raise one finger in the air if I needed to pee, or two for a bowel movement.

Sometimes you held your aching arm in the air for ages, bursting to go but desperately trying to hold on until someone deigned to notice. If a teacher didn't like you they often pretended not to see you on purpose, getting twisted fun from a child's discomfort. Asking to go when there were lots of people about, such as in school or at mealtimes, was so embarrassing. I hated having to use my fingers to announce to a roomful of my classmates what it was I needed to do.

Some time ago Grandpa had stated in a newsletter that children should be able to go eight hours during the night without needing the toilet. Asking to go at night got you a beating, so the only option was to hold on as best you could. The agony of trying to sleep with a full bladder was awful. But if you wet the bed you got a beating too. It wasn't much of a choice – ask and get hit, wet the bed and get hit. The first time that happened to me I spent a sleepless night on cold, wet sheets, ashamed and afraid, dreading morning and the inevitable public humiliation.

The initial sense of safety I had felt in the first few weeks after moving to Bangkok quickly dissipated. I began to show clear signs of disturbed behaviour. At dinner I stole a knife from the dining hall and hid it under my pillow until bedtime when I took it out and carved Clay's name into the wooden frame of my bunk.

Uncle Titus caught me. Without a word he dragged me into the toilet next door and went at me with the fly-swat. He hit me so hard I fell over. He ordered me to stand up and he hit me again. I collapsed against the wall. This time as I struggled up he ordered me to hold onto the towel rail for support. I gripped the rail so tight my fingers went white as blow after blow rained down on my bare buttocks. If I cried out he followed with a harder hit. I bit my lip so hard my tooth went right through it, making it bleed. When it was finally over I couldn't walk.

As quickly as a light switch turning on, Titus's violent rage turned to gentle concern. He picked me up, carried me onto my bunk and carefully placed me on the bed. He stroked my hair, wet with my tears, away from my face and shook his head. When he spoke it was in a low, sad voice, as if he was the one who was in agony. 'Natacha, I did not enjoy that. Why did you make me do that? Why did you put me through the pain of hurting you? Do you know why I just spanked you? I spanked you for Jesus. Jesus loves you. I spanked you for your own good and to help you become a better little girl. You were a bad girl but Jesus wants you to be a good girl. Together we are going to help you do that. Do you understand why I had to hurt you? It was to help you.'

I nodded.

'Now give me a cuddle and say thank you.' He had tears in his eyes.

Hugging the man who had just beaten me senseless was the last thing I wanted to do, but I wrapped my arms around his neck, placed a kiss on his cheek and mustered up a watery smile.

'Thank you very much for helping me, Uncle Titus.'

'Now let us pray to Jesus for forgiveness and thank him for this special time we have had together.'

It was normal to have to hug and pray with the person who had beaten you. They made out it was for your own good. If you refused the post-beating cuddle you risked another, so you smiled sweetly and said nothing. It was how the game was played.

So many of the adults seemed to take pure delight in their power to punish us, perfecting their own versions of torture methods for children. Older children got what was called the board – a plank of wood drilled with holes. As it swung to hit you air rushed through the holes, which made it sting more. In a sadistic twist, children were often thrown into the shower first. The board on a wet bottom was excruciating. Many poor kids faced that at least once a week.

Aside from my three little friends I was not a popular child. I was skinny, with scraggly thin hair and freckles – an obvious target for bullying. There was a girl one year older than me called Honey. For some reason she took an instant dislike to me. Every day she found new ways to taunt me, whether it was nipping my arms as she brushed past, dropping my books onto the floor or kicking me from behind in class. She was an angelic-looking little girl with long dark curls and chocolate saucers for eyes. All the adults thought she was adorable. I don't think I ever saw her once get the swat. But her skills as a manipulator meant she was certainly responsible for several other kids getting it.

One evening in the mess hall she picked up my dinner plate, pretending to smell it, then spat in it. This went unnoticed to anyone but me, of course. She gave me a little smirk of satisfaction. I glared at her, promising myself that this time I would have my revenge.

My opportunity came a few days later. It was monsoon season and during a break from the downpours the teachers let us out to play for half an hour. I found a large hairy grub on a bush and placed it in my pocket. After nap time I made sure I was the last child in the line, hanging back for just a few seconds – long enough to open her drawer and throw the grub inside. I spent the rest of the day feeling nervously self-satisfied. At bedtime I was really looking forward to the moment she discovered it. But she didn't. I went to sleep disappointed, and by the time I woke up had forgotten all about it.

At lunch we were told to prepare ourselves to write an 'Open Heart Report' before dinner. Both adults and children did these once a week, although in other communes they were done daily. In theirs the adults had to fill out a form detailing the sharing, writing down the full details of who they had sex with and on what nights. They were supposed to write it all up in unexpurgated detail, saying what positions they did, whether they had full sex, oral sex or just foreplay. The reports were passed on to the Shepherds, who dished out any relevant punishments and sent edited versions on to David Berg. It wasn't unusual for someone to later see their reports referred to in a Mo letter, either as good examples or through naming and shaming anyone who came across as a doubter.

For children, the reports were just as bizarre. We had to write down what bad thoughts or spiritual battles we'd had and any moral lessons or victories we'd learned that week. We also got asked about our toilet habits – how many poos we'd done and whether they were soft or hard. Sometimes, after the Home Shepherd or your teacher had reviewed your report they would take you out on a 'walkie talkie', which was usually a walk around the garden, during which they would discuss points from your report, particularly those relating to your NWOs (Need Work On) – a list of areas you admitted you needed to work on, for example trying to be more humble or less selfish.

But the reports weren't just about ourselves. We also had to include any unspiritual or bad behaviour we'd seen other kids do.

The teacher went round every child asking them to admit verbally to anything naughty they had done or thought. If you didn't admit to something you were called a liar. So it was easier just to confess something – anything. That was horrible enough. But what was far more unpredictable was what others said. It wasn't in my nature to get others into trouble. I had too much empathy, especially with the naughty kids or the cry-baby ones. But if you went for more than two sessions claiming you hadn't seen anyone do anything bad you were accused of hiding something or covering up for someone. So you were left with the choice of a telling a blatant lie or saying something as mild as you could get away with. I usually opted for the latter and prayed that what I said wouldn't land another child a serious beating. Other children, like Honey, relished it. She never failed to take the opportunity to twist and exaggerate a tiny misdeed out of all proportion.

It didn't occur to me to be worried about the grub. I definitely knew I hadn't been spotted putting it in the drawer. But of course I hadn't bargained on the fact that little snitches like Honey have eyes in the back of their heads. She had seen me pocket the grub in the garden and carry it into the house. The first words out of her mouth at the reporting session were: 'Natacha put a dirty thing in her pocket.'

I flustered for a few minutes, pretending it wasn't true. But my face gave it away.

Of course picking up a garden pest and putting it in your jeans wasn't the greatest crime in the scheme of things, and this time even the teacher could see that. I might well have escaped a spanking but for my own complete inability to be devious. Before I could stop them the words blurted out of my stupid mouth: 'I put it in Honey's drawer. I'm sorry.'

The pain of the beating was only slightly lessened by the joy of hearing Honey's squeal when the teacher dragged us both into the dorm and opened the drawer. The big fat grey grub was sitting there on her favourite blouse.

But if I had thought the worst thing Bangkok could throw at me was crazy rules and punishments like the plank and the wall, I was wrong – far worse was to come.

I had recently learned that the little girl with the braided hair on the cover of *Heaven's Girl* was in fact inspired by Grandpa's real granddaughter, Mene.

Grandpa often referred to her as Merry Mene in his letters. She was one of his favourite grandkids and lived with him. Of course I still didn't know where that was because the location still needed to be kept a strict secret so that the Antichrist couldn't find him and kill him.

Once I learned Mene *was* Heaven's Girl she became my real-life heroine. I imagined her running through forests zapping people with her special powers. If I could have chosen to meet any of Grandpa's family in real life it would have been her. But the mere mention of the name Davidito, his adopted heir, still brought me out in a jealous rage. The fact he was a boy probably didn't help. I way preferred the idea of a princess instead of a prince leading me into the fight at Armageddon.

Uncle Titus called us into the dining room for group devotion time. He stood in the centre of the room with a thick sheaf of papers in his hand. 'I have something very important to read today', he intoned in his low voice. 'The whole family is here because this is an issue that affects all of us. There are many reports of second-generation family members behaving in ungodly or ungrateful ways. This will not be tolerated.'

He explained that in his hand were a series of letters Grandpa had written about Mene. As she reached her teens she had started calling up demons. Every night the demons came to possess her and trick her into being naughty. She saw demons everywhere; she talked to them and even invited them into her bed. Grandpa had tried so hard to make the demons leave Mene. He had carried out exorcisms where he prayed over her as much as 50 times a day and had been forced to beat her up with a big stick. Sometimes the exorcisms made her faint or throw up, but Grandpa said this was a very good thing because it proved the demons were leaving her body.

I stood to attention, listening in stunned silence. Uncle Titus continued in his pained-sounding voice.

'I am going to pass around copies of another letter. I want you all to read it carefully. As you will see it is a recording of a real conversation between Grandpa and Mene. You will see with your own eyes how much Grandpa loves her and wants to save her.'

With shaky hands I looked down at the sheet of paper.

It began with the explanation that Grandpa had handed Mene a large rod and asked her to feel 'how heavy it is'.

Then he and Mene spoke back and forth: 'Slap her! Slap her good! Knock her around! Let her have it! The Lord took hold of her head … and yanked it around and back and forth until I was afraid I was going to yank her head off or break her neck! God was so angry … And then I hauled her and slapped her, I don't know how many times tonight, hard, right?'

'Yes, sir.'

Mene didn't seem to be answering back, pretty much just saying 'Yes, sir' in agreement. But that didn't seem to be enough for him. He ordered Mama Maria and Sara to tie Mene to her bed without food and water, for days if needed. 'I don't care if you wet the bed, dear, your hands are going to be tied to the sides of that bed at night. If you don't get rid of those demons, you may have to get whipped in bed, caned in bed.'

After we had finished reading you could have heard a pin drop. Every single child in the room was stunned into their own silent world of terror by what they had just read. The piece of paper in my hand felt so tainted. I wanted to tear it up.

'So, children,' said Titus, 'Grandpa has sent us some very important lessons today. Some of you in this house are reaching this same tender age where demons will also come to test you. Do not to be tempted to make Mene's mistake by calling them up and playing with those demons. Do you hear me? Reject the demons. Reject them! I want to hear you promise Jesus. Say it. We *will* reject the demons.'

Clearly worried voices recited back: 'We *will* reject the demons.'

It got worse. Titus said what we'd just read was not in fact the end of the story. It had been written some time ago. But Mene had not heeded her lessons. She had continued to trick poor Grandpa with her pretty face and sweet ways by pretending to be cured, while all the time secretly bringing more demons into his home.

As a last resort to help her learn the error of her ways Grandpa set up a special school for her on a very remote island. To keep her company he had sent other naughty, evil children to join her. They were what were called DTs, detention teens. If any of us tried the same tricks we too would be sent there. But even the school hadn't worked for Mene. Grandpa could see now she was simply a hopeless case – a plaything of the devil himself.

For days after hearing all this I felt nauseous. I got on my knees and prayed extra hard, asking Jesus to help me be really good and not fall foul of evil like Mene. I felt completely betrayed by her. How could my heroine have trusted the devil and let him into her heart? I was so angry with her that if she'd been in front of me I think I would have wanted to beat her too.

But Merry Mene wasn't the only problem for the group. The original group (back when it was known as the Children of God) had been formed in 1968, over 20 years ago. The first tranche of babies born in those early days had reached their teens a few years earlier. Ever since then reports had been reaching the Shepherds of teenagers getting into fights, rebelling, drinking alcohol or, worst of all, trying to escape the communes. The leadership saw a crisis on their hands. Without getting the situation under control it was feared younger kids would start to follow suit.

In Word Time we were read countless more Mo letters about the problems of 'teen terror'. There was story after story of 'ungrateful, ungodly' children who had failed to appreciate the 'loving family' they had been born into.

Eventually we were told Grandpa had set up special camps, called Victor Camps or TTCs (Teen Training Centres), to fix the problem. Young teens would be sent to them *before* they had a chance to turn bad. In the camps they would do a combination of physical labour, prayer and fasting. That would help them stay on the path of righteousness and ensure they didn't follow the bad examples of others.

Once again rules made by leaders far away tore apart my family. Now aged 12, my eldest brother, Joe, was sent to a TTC. My dad promised him that it would be great fun and that he'd get to do lots of activities and sports to help him grow strong. The look of dread on his face as he kissed my parents goodbye told me he didn't believe a word of it.

Less than a week after Joe was sent away my father announced we were moving to a different commune. I couldn't wait.

Chapter 9

From Russia with Love

I climbed up onto the closed toilet seat. I knew if I leaned forward onto the windowsill and stretched up onto my toes I could see out to the gate. I stared longingly – praying, willing the gate to open and for my mother to walk through it.

'Natacha. Natacha, where are you, naughty girl?'

At the sound of Aunty Esther's voice I jumped off the toilet and ran to take my seat in class.

As I slid into my chair Esther's fist rapped into the side of my temple. 'Wicked girl.'

Four months earlier we'd moved communes. Initially I had thought the move might make my life easier, but as it turned out I was sadly mistaken. This house was even bigger than the last, with between 150 and 200 permanent residents. On the surface it appeared to be a lot more comfortable than the previous one, with a pretty garden laid to lawn and planted with coconut trees. There was a square-shaped outdoor swimming pool, which I had been thrilled to discover we were allowed to use once a week for physical education lessons. But if the previous commune had been a madhouse of weird regulations, this one was like a military prison camp. Children wore uniforms depending on their age; all the outfits had been donated from various sources and were a funny hotchpotch of styles. I was seven now and the girls in my age group wore a uniform of a short skirt with a drawstring blouse, which was made of a horrible synthetic nylon that felt either cold or clammy on my skin depending on whether I was standing under a fan or outside in the heat.

As in the home before, we walked everywhere in silence, but if anything the school routine was even more rigid. Classes were held in a separate annex with different teachers for different subjects. For Word Time I had two teachers, Esther and Jeremiah, an African-American married couple from New York.

They were as different as chalk and cheese. Jeremiah loved children. He was a gentle giant with a shaved head who made up silly poems to make us laugh and always seemed to know if one of us was feeling down or poorly. He was the first adult I had trusted since Joy had left me and I absolutely adored him. Esther was rotund, as short as he was tall, and with a huge Afro that was almost as wide as her. Her favoured method of communication was a hit around the back of the head with knuckles as hard as steel. I hated her.

My father had been far less happy since the move, having now been officially demoted. The management backbiting against him that had been brewing since Leah's departure had got gradually worse, until eventually he was told his services as a Shepherd were no longer required. He was utterly dejected, having worked hard to climb the internal hierarchy since joining. To be removed from his post so casually was like a slap in the face. The few freedoms his seniority had allowed him, such as travel to other homes or having a say in the work my mother did, disappeared overnight.

But for the five children remaining at home, Matt, Marc, Vincent, Guy and me, this meant we saw much more of him. I missed Joe but I had seen so little of him in the previous commune anyway that his absence didn't seem so strange. His removal to the Victor Camp had been much harder on my mother, who was wracked with guilt, not that she had much choice in the matter.

Two months after we moved he had been allowed a long-weekend visit home. On the Sunday, family day, we spent it as always in my parents' bedroom, but instead of jabbering and organising noisy games of marbles as normal he sat on the end of the bed looking subdued and rigid. We asked questions about the camp and the things they did there. He answered politely but briefly.

'Do you like it there?' my dad asked. 'I mean, it is fun like I said it would be? Right?'

Joe was staring at the floor. 'Yes, Dad. Sure. We have fun.' He didn't look up.

It was hard to put a finger on it. He just seemed – different.

After dinner the bus came to pick him up. It had done the rounds of the other nearby communes first so it was already crammed full with miserable-looking teenagers when it got to us. Without a word Joe got on and took a seat.

As my mother waved goodbye the kindly Jeremiah noticed she was upset. He patted her on the shoulder. 'Are you OK, Patience? It must be a challenge to say goodbye.'

She glanced around. Jeremiah's concern was genuine. The other eyes watching her were not. Her every gesture was being assessed for a negative reaction.

She gave a brittle little smile. 'No, no, it's a blessing. Truly. I am so thankful for it.' She turned to go back inside, trying not to let them see her cry.

Vincent, now four, was growing into a naughtier child by the day. The commune aunties and uncles had little patience for what they saw as his spoilt, whining ways. He was smacked and hit often. One uncle hit him so hard with the back of his shoe that he was left badly bruised, and he cried non-stop for three days.

Perhaps the pain of Joe's absence was still raw, or maybe it was the fact that she was hormonal, having recently learned she was pregnant again, but something made my usually submissive mother snap as her maternal instinct kicked in. She demanded to speak to a senior Shepherd and put in a formal complaint about the man.

Instead of supporting a woman, quite rightfully angry at the unacceptable levels of violence meted out to her small son, the Shepherd backed the uncle's version of events. Mom was labelled a troublemaker and a potential doubter.

To prevent her 'backsliding' even further she was ordered to join a team of pioneers on a mission to Siberia in the Soviet Union. The team was to assess whether the Soviet Union, which was in political turmoil at the end of the Cold War, was 'sheepy' – believing – enough for The Family to set up bases there. Their mission was to try to win over new recruits, hold Bible classes and see if they could find wealthy patrons who would help support a commune financially.

At the next family day she and my dad announced the bad news.

'It's a great honour for her to have been asked,' said my dad, somewhat unconvincingly.

'But why does Mommy have to go away?' Vincent was sitting on her lap, his tearful face buried in her chest. 'Don't you love us, Mommy?'

'Oh, my little one. Of course I do. I love you so, so, so much. But Jesus has asked me to do this special favour for him. The people there need his love and I have to go share it with them. If Jesus needs this from me, then we all have to make a little sacrifice, don't we?'

She cupped his face in her hands to make him look at her. 'Jesus needs me, Vincent. For him, who gives us so much love, we have to give ourselves. It won't be for long, little one.'

She and Dad exchanged another of their secret looks.

Later I heard them arguing. It sounded as though Mom was finding this easier than Dad. 'You are pregnant. I have got to find a way to prevent this.'

She hissed at him: 'Marcel, shush. Keep your voice down. If someone overhears you'll be reported too. And then what? I need you here to take care of the children. I will manage. If it's Jesus's will to keep me safe then I will fine.'

'How in Jesus's name can a pregnant woman be sent to such a godforsaken place? This is not about Jesus. It's about punishing us both. I won't have it.'

She went over and put her arms around him. 'If this is God's will then we will survive this test. It's only for 12 weeks. It will fly by. And when I come back Jesus will reward us with another baby.'

He nodded at her wanly.

What my father knew but we children didn't was that she was being sent close to the city of Chelyabinsk, the site of a former Soviet plutonium production site and one of the most polluted places on earth.

My father was beside himself with worry. He also felt incredibly guilty. He had fully supported her complaint and encouraged her to do it. So he felt that if anyone should be have been punished it should be him. He pleaded with the Shepherds to reconsider, but to no avail. This plummeted him into a severe depression.

My youngest brother, Guy, wasn't yet two years old. He had never been separated from my mom for more than a day, having always slept in the nursery where she worked. The day she left his heart-rending cries of 'Mommy, Mommy, wan' my mommy' rang out through the corridors. I watched as an aunty picked him up to cuddle him, but instead of calming or reassuring him that his mother was coming back she repeated over and over the same old motivational mantra that was supposed to cure everything: 'Get the victory, get the victory.'

How was that supposed to comfort a two year old whose mother has been ripped away from him? I decided I would look after him and take my mom's place until she came back.

That was easier said than done because usually I only got to see him on family day. Every chance I got I invented an excuse to sneak out of class and dash into the nursery to pick him up for a cuddle or sing him a little song. The aunties who made up the nursery staff were generally sympathetic and didn't tell tales on me, but I rarely got away with it and usually received one of Esther's knuckle punches when I got back to class.

I didn't care how much she hurt me. Guy was all that mattered. On family days I did my best to cheer up my dad, telling silly jokes to try to make him laugh. I tried my best to hold my own unhappiness in, saving it for those secret moments in the bathroom when I climbed onto the toilet and said a little prayer for the gate to open and for her to walk in.

Increasingly, performing troupes were seen as a really effective way to bring in funds. This was especially true in Thailand where a troupe of Western performers had big novelty value. The commune had a professional-sounding troupe who were booked up weeks in advance to perform at office parties, in shopping malls, orphanages and even adult prisons. The troupe played a mixed set of songs, dance routines and funny sketches. Both my parents were extremely musical and had passed on the love of performing to me and my brothers.

My singing voice was very pretty but I wasn't a brilliant dancer. However, I was determined to land myself a starring role in the upcoming Christmas show. The troupe had been booked by a big shopping mall to perform for a full two weeks in the run up to the holidays. The mall was popular with tourists so the thought of playing to such a large audience was thrilling.

I wanted to make my mom proud of me when she came back. I also badly needed something to distract me from missing her so much.

Part of the show involved a nativity. I was desperate to be cast as Mary or an angel, the plum roles all the little girls wanted. I auditioned but of course those parts went to the prettiest girls. Instead I got cast as a villager. I was disappointed but consoled that I got to be part of a big group dance scene. I spent every moment I could rehearsing my steps. Everyone took it very seriously and I was determined to do a good job.

In early December, just a week before the show was due to start, I was pulled aside for a 'quiet chat' at rehearsal by Uncle Matthew, the director. I knew I'd messed up a few steps and braced myself for an angry dressing down.

Matthew didn't mince his words. 'You are out of the troupe. You need to join the Minnies programme. Succeed and there might be a place for you next year.'

The Minnies was a fattening-up programme for too-skinny kids. The Family didn't want hungry or sick-looking children being seen in public for fear the authorities might get concerned and investigate conditions. It seems I had fallen below the acceptable weight. It wasn't surprising considering the poor-quality food and tiny portions we were dished out. And it wasn't my fault I was so thin. But being kicked out of the show felt like the hardest punishment of all. I was shattered, crying myself to sleep every night. To make it worse the other girls teased me, showing off their costumes and never missing an opportunity to tell me how excited they were about being in the show.

To fatten me up I was placed on a regime of two daily portions of stodgy rice porridge with sugar and milk powder, in addition to my normal meals. It was so thick a spoon would stand up in it. At first the sugar rush felt like quite a treat and I enjoyed it. But after weeks of eating it every day I only had to look at a bowl and I would want to throw up.

The week before Christmas I became almost as depressed as my father. Without the show to distract me my mother's absence became unbearable. My father consoled himself and all of us with the constant reassurance that the three months were almost up and she'd be home in the New Year.

Then I found him crying in his room. 'Jesus sent a prophecy, Natacha. Mom is doing such good work there that he needs her to stay longer. Maybe another three months.'

His voice cracked as he said the words. I ran over and hugged him, trying to squeeze him tightly with my arms to make him feel better.

Christmas Day was awful. We woke up to the usual regimented prayers and taped Mo sermons. Every child in the commune, whatever their age, got the same present – a packet of crayons and an orange. In the afternoon we were given special family time. Guy cried, my father snapped at him and Vincent and I tried to play as quietly as possible with our new crayons. Every one of us was completely miserable without Mom.

In mid-January some of our donors came for a visit. These were the owners of a nearby chicken farm who occasionally donated boxes of eggs to us. I don't know if they acted out of pure kindness or whether they received something in return, but visitors to a commune were a rare event, and this sent many of the adults into a tailspin. How we were perceived by the outside world was paramount. Letting anyone walk away with the idea that The Family was anything less than perfect was to be prevented at all costs. Any kids who looked sick were hidden in one of the bedrooms. By then I'd put on enough weight to be deemed OK to be seen.

The Shepherd dispatched Jeremiah to go into town to buy biscuits and bottles of cola (things that were deemed system food and usually strictly banned). It was pure torture as we were wheeled out in our best dresses and presented to the visitors. My mouth salivated as one of our guests picked up a sugar-coated biscuit and dunked it into his tea. But I knew better than to ask for one, and there was no way to grab one in secret.

When they left we were all instructed to stand in the garden and sing them a goodbye song. As we sang two aunties were already scooping up the leftover biscuits, putting them in a lockable tin and into a bolted cupboard. When we came back inside there was nothing, not even a crumb to salvage.

The next day at breakfast I watched in horror as Vincent was dragged to the front of the dining room, had his trousers pulled down and was publicly spanked with the swat. Somehow, between the song and the guests leaving, he had managed to grab a half-opened packet of biscuits and stuff them in his pocket.

Perhaps what certain adults sensed in Vincent was his innate sense of justice. That may explain why so many of them struggled with him. Instead of sneaking off to greedily eat the biscuits himself he had distributed one each to the other kids in his dorm. His reasoning for doing so was sweetly innocent, but by the standards under which we lived it made him something close to a seditious agitator. As he gave each child their biscuit he had said: 'We are children; we need biscuits.'

But if adults didn't know what to make of him, other children loved him. He had a special depth of character that other kids sensed was important, even if they didn't know why. If anyone else had handed out stolen biscuits they would have been reported or told on, but not him. He only got caught because he had two biscuits left over which he'd hidden under his pillow ready to eat during the night. Aunty Esther found them in a spot bed inspection. As Esther turned puce at this most heinous of discoveries Vincent didn't flinch. Instead he calmly held out his hands with the biscuits on his palm.

'If you don't punish me you may have them,' he offered.

For the deep-thinking little boy this was perfectly logical. But within commune rules attempting to bribe others was akin to mind poisoning, which is why he was made such a public example of.

My own sense of justice was beginning to be aroused too, by a boy called James. He was in his pre-teens and severely disabled. He couldn't walk and made noises instead of talking. His head and legs shook uncontrollably when he moved and he always had a little line of spittle coming out of his mouth. Most of the other children were scared of him and didn't want to go anywhere near him.

The adults said he was possessed by demons and told us that is why he was that way.

In the mornings James was washed and dressed, then tied to a chair to keep him still as he was force-fed porridge. If he refused to eat it an uncle would stand behind him, gripping his head and forcing his mouth open, while an aunty shovelled porridge inside with a spoon. Then his jaw was clamped shut until he swallowed it down.

If he wasn't tied up he used to punch himself in the face or bang his head against the wall, so he was made to wear boxing gloves that were taped down so that he couldn't take them off. Then if the weather wasn't too scorching or wet he was put out in the garden for the day, usually tied to a tree. He often screamed out and made terrible wild animal howls. When he did that someone was sent outside to hit him. If he refused to stop they either shoved a dry nappy in his mouth or dragged him back inside to lock him in the tiny room where he slept. It was right at the back of the house, like a dungeon with a tiny barred window and no air conditioning.

The worst thing was when he had seizures and fell to the floor writhing and banging. 'The devil is in him again,' the adults would shout, rushing over to hold him down, punch and slap him and say prayers over him, urging the evil inside him to cast itself out.

I didn't know what was wrong with him but I could see he was a boy, not a demon. James's eyes were so confused and full of pain I didn't understand how anyone could think he was bad. He reminded me of my earlier childhood friend Simon with his taped-up mouth.

He was a bit like a communal punch bag. Other kids were often tasked with feeding him and would get frustrated at him, following the adults' lead by giving him a kick or a slap round the head.

His younger half-sister Claire was my closest friend. She and I were the only ones who were kind to him, holding his hands for a few grabbed seconds or whispering to him that he was a good boy and not to cry. Claire confided in me that when he was born the leaders accused her mother of allowing the devil into her bed, insisting that James's disability could only be the result of an unholy union with evil. Claire confided in me that she sometimes wished he could just go straight to heaven to stop him suffering so much.

Early spring came, and with it the beginning of the rainy season. The pain of my mother's absence hadn't lessened, but I had learned to cope by blocking it out as much as I could, focusing instead on the males of the family by trying to mother them all.

But, lying in bed, I was often overcome with a sense of panic. Thérèse and Leah had never come back. Was my mom really ever coming home? Was Dad lying to me when he said she was?

When I thought these thoughts I struggled to breathe and my old shakes came back. Uncle Jeremiah seemed to sense my fear and played a huge part in seeing me through that difficult time. He always made a point of talking about her or praising me, saying how pleased she would be at how clever I had become or how she would like a picture I had drawn. His concern for me meant the world.

The air was sticky and the skies fat with tropical thunder when the gates finally opened and a beige sedan car with blacked-out windows drove in. It was just after lunch and I was filing back to class when I heard the sound of the engine.

My heart went tight in my chest. Could it be? I hardly dared move in case it wasn't. Then I heard Vincent's squeal of delight: 'Mommy's here!'

I broke away from the line and ran outside just as the door opened. For a second I barely recognised her. She was fat and round and heavily pregnant. As a joke she had put on a big furry Russian hat that made her look like a doll.

'Mommy, Mommy, Mommy yaaaayyyy, Mommy is here!'

By now Dad, Matt and Marc were outside too. We all threw ourselves at her at once. She giggled with delight, not knowing whom to hug first. My dad had carried Guy down from the nursery. He was wary and looked scared as my father held him forward: 'Look, baby, your mommy is here. It's your mommy. You know Mommy.'

Guy shook his head and clung around my dad's neck.

'Oh Marcel, why?' she whispered under her breath. 'My own baby doesn't know me.'

He nodded wordlessly, biting down on his lip.

She was supposed to have come back from her mission compliant and uncomplaining. Showing any public signs of anger or regret at having been cruelly ripped away from her children could land her in trouble again. So, a bit like the forced cuddles we had to face after a beating, my mom too had to spend the next few days playing a pretend game, whereby she made out the pioneer camp had been a *just wonderful time* and how *grateful* she'd been for the opportunity.

On her first family day back at home she sat me on the bed with a huge smile. 'I have something very special for you, *chérie*. I bet you will never guess what it is.'

With a dramatic flourish she presented the most beautiful, prettiest, most wondrous thing I had ever seen. It was a Barbie doll, dressed in Russian-style clothes. The doll wore an embroidered little tunic, black trousers, plastic lace-up boots and a little furry hat like the one my mom had.

I squealed with delight, kissing the doll. Mom put a finger to her lips. 'Shhhh. Keep her to yourself. She's your special toy, so look after her well. Please do not brag.'

She was giving me a tacit warning. As a rule we didn't have toys. There were a few shared ones around but they were generally simple and educational, building blocks or alphabet games. Things like dolls were said to set a bad moral example and were a sign of rampant commerciality. My mother knew she was taking another risk by giving it to me.

I tried to hide my Barbie well, cramming her into the space between my mattress and the bunk frame. But I kept sneaking her out to look at her during the night. I was so mesmerised by her that I didn't notice another girl had spotted me.

Of course, she complained about me. After breakfast next morning Aunty Esther came to take my doll away. I tried so hard not to give up her hiding place. 'Where is it?' Esther demanded, waving a warning fist.

I sat on the bed, shaking my head. 'I don't know.' For the first time I was finding lying easy.

Esther pulled up the sheets, shook out the pillows, her eyes as manic as a bloodhound in pursuit of prey. 'Tell me now, you naughty girl. Where is it?'

I shook my head, lips pursed, and refused to utter another word.

In the end it was inevitable she'd lift up the mattress to look underneath. With a triumphant shriek she brandished the doll in the air like a trophy. 'This is going in the trash right now.'

She walked out, muttering curses about my mother. 'What was the woman thinking, bringing such wordliness into the good Lord's house?'

The unjustness of it all left me too full of impotent rage to even cry.

I put my hand in my sock and pulled out a little trophy of my own – Barbie's fur hat.

Chapter 10

Mutiny at Tea

'Go, go, go. The soldiers are at the door. They are right here. Move it. MOVE IT!'

I leapt out of my bunk, trying to adjust my eyes to the darkness. A cold wave of fear flooded through me but I knew I had to stay calm and follow the drill. I fumbled for my flee bag – a little brown satchel with stitched pockets that held a clean set of clothes, my torch and a tin of food. I sprinted out of the room, past the angry monkeys that lived in the garden, and towards the surrounding forest and the secret clearing that was our designated meeting point. Had the war begun? I ran as fast as I could, trying to keep up with the older children in front of me, leaping over fallen branches and tearing leafy vegetation out of my eyes. At the clearing I was relieved to see my parents and brothers there waiting.

'Natacha. Thank God.' My dad let out a sigh of relief.

I ran over and hugged them. My father carried a briefcase with our passports and birth certificates; he also wore a rucksack with food and useful items like rope, matches and sleeping bags. My mother had a smaller rucksack containing her and my father's clothes, a first aid kit and a torch. Between us all we covered the basics we would need to survive for a few days in the wilderness or until we could reach proper shelter.

Everyone had faces turned towards the trees, scanning every shadow for signs of movement, preparing for the moment of attack.

'Is this it?' asked Marc in a scared voice.

I got into position, planting my feet on the ground a few inches apart, shoulders back, head sideways. Narrowing my eyes I tried to shoot a thunderbolt. Nothing happened. I summoned up all my powers of concentration and tried again, willing my eyes to work. Nothing.

Surely my superpower would be working if the war had really started?

For the next two hours we waited there in silence, tense and alert, ready for the order to disperse and run. When the soldiers attacked we knew what to do. The group would split up and run in different directions to confuse them. Some people would be able to get away but those who were killed early on would be doing the others a great service by allowing them precious seconds to escape. Families were told to separate, to let the strongest get away. But my parents were adamant that whatever happened we would stay together. Matt was to hold Vincent's hand. Marc was to hold Guy's. I was to hold my father's. Under no circumstances were we to let go of each other until we found a hiding place.

If we survived the initial attack there was no going home afterwards – it was all-out war. That meant running through forests, hiding in caves, plotting rebellions – doing whatever we could to weaken the forces of the Antichrist until the final battle of Armageddon.

Eventually, Uncle Isaiah, an Irish former merchant seaman, took a few steps away from the group before turning to face us.

'Stand down. Drill over,' he announced. I wanted to burst into tears and hit him. Hours of adrenalin-filled anxiety, for what?

'Well done everyone. Response time is up on the last drill. But there is plenty of room for improvement. When it's the real thing we won't get a second chance.'

We filed back into the house in silence. No war today, just more practice.

I was almost ten now. We'd just moved to Malaysia. It was 1993, the year God had told Grandpa the End Time would begin with the start of the Great Tribulation; that was the seven years of war that would be the precursor to the second coming of Jesus and the great and final battle of Armageddon. We woke up every day expecting, in many ways hoping, for it to start. It was our very reason for existing.

School lessons had pretty much been completely given over to war preparations. We were told that the Tribulation wars had already begun in many parts of the world. The USA and Europe, especially the countries of France, Germany and Great Britain, were already lost, and completely under the devil's control. Famine and disaster had all but destroyed the great man-made cities of New York, Paris, Berlin and London. I remembered when Joy had shown me pictures of collapsed buildings and dead flowers. I felt really sad for the system people, especially the children. They should have saved themselves in time, but they didn't. They didn't listen to our prophet, and because of that their children would go hungry and live in war.

We prepared for the secret missions we might need to undertake during the long months of fighting. For example I was warned I might need to go undercover, pretending to be a policeman to get information. Or I might have to steal food from a supermarket, in which case wearing a disguise like sunglasses and a hat was important to fool the system cameras.

Aunty Sunshine gave us a special talk one day. She was Malaysian, and because she had a unique understanding of the world outside our gates, as she spoke the language, she was always chosen to go on the really dangerous missions to buy food.

'Look, children. This is the wig I wear.'

It was a long mass of blonde curls. She bent forward, pulled it onto her head and stood up again, sliding it into place.

We were very impressed.

'And these are my "systemite" glasses. These are very important so that nobody can see where my eyes are looking.'

She slipped on a pair of black wrap-around sunglasses.

'And last, but not least, my hat.'

It was a blue cap with a plastic visor emblazoned with a red love heart and the words, 'I love New York.'

'I need to wear these things to blend in with the systemite people. Some of the nice gentle ones, the ones we call sheep, would not hurt me. But those we call the goats, the disbelievers and the decadent sodomite ones, might capture and torture me. If I didn't have my disguise they would recognise me as one of God's chosen ones and kill me. This wig, hat and glasses are Grandpa's clever way of protecting me.'

Grandpa was increasingly concerned for all of us. He sent the children a special letter called 'Victory in Babylon' that warned about the forces of the Antichrist and the possibility of raids by authorities. He said we could be snatched away by government people claiming to help us. The only chance we had to survive in that situation was to remain absolutely silent and not answer any of their questions, no matter how nice they might pretend to be or with how much delicious food or fun toys they might tempt us. Grandpa was very clear – it was all a trap designed to ensnare us.

Impending death and destruction were everywhere. My parents talked about it constantly. I was anxious but it was so normalised I wasn't that scared. I did start to think about getting killed again and wondering how much it would hurt. Would it be slow or fast? Would the killer taunt me and say horrible things? Or would they feel bad and say sorry? Would I get shot, raped, burned to death or stabbed? I went through every form of violent death I could think of, trying to prepare myself for how I would react when it happened.

When we relocated to Malaysia, Joe had to remain in Thailand at the Victor Camp. We had barely heard anything from him since his brief visit home. My mom was worried sick and didn't want to move without him. I overheard her fighting with my dad about it in angry whispers.

'How can we even think about going to a new country without our son?' she argued.

Dad's voice was reassuring but with a firm tone that didn't allow for dissent. 'The teens in those camps will be having the time of their lives, playing lots of sports and climbing trees. These are the things that boys of that age need to do. Besides, the war is coming. Maybe they will all be safer there.'

Mom was still recovering from her Siberian experience and I suspect she was too scared to keep rocking the boat. If we asked about her time there she generally fobbed us off with descriptions of deep snow and how if you didn't wear a woolly scarf over your face when you went outside your lungs would freeze. Any deeper questions were batted away. I suspected some very bad things had happened to her but I knew better than to keep pushing.

In May of that year, a few weeks after we arrived, my little sister Aimée was born. Having another baby girl thrilled both my parents and lifted my father out of his depression. I was completely delighted to finally have another sister, especially as by now I assumed I had lost Thérèse forever.

The new commune was in Penang, an island off the coast of Malaysia, not far from the border with Thailand. It was a wild, untamed landscape with lots of fern-covered hills. Our new garden backed straight onto the edge of a large expanse of jungle, which was full of scary wild animals.

The commune was what was known as a 'selah' home, which meant that it was a small secret home that would pretend to be made up of normal families in order to fool the systemites. It acted as a kind of bed and breakfast for visiting members from Thailand, who needed to leave the country in order to renew their visas.

There were 30 permanent residents – four families and a handful of single adults.

Vincent was now seven and in the MCs (middle children) dorm with me. It was brilliant being able to share a room with him, but our joy at that was marred by our teacher, Isaiah. He was a madman, and as he had been in the merchant navy was obsessed with everything military. He ran our dorm like a ship – he was Captain, his three sons Sean, Seamus and Seafra were First Officers, and Vincent and I were lowly deck mates. As soon as we woke up Isaiah had us on physical duties, scrubbing the wooden floorboards with coarse brushes.

'Swab those decks,' he shouted. 'I want her shipshape and battle ready.'

If we didn't scrub fast enough he would snatch the brush from our hands and fling it at our backs. Normally you had just enough time to cover your head before the wooden brush slapped into your shoulder blades or, worse, spine.

If he was feeling particularly vicious he would force you face down onto the ground, grab your ankles in one hand and wrists in the other, then force them up over your back with your tummy pressed hard into the floor.

'Time for a keelhauling.'

The pain it caused your stomach and organs was immense.

'This navy runs on discipline. I'll make sailors of you yet.'

Uncle Isaiah hated any sign of weakness or improper attitude. But most of all Isaiah hated Vincent. And that feeling was mutual.

We had been out on survival training for most of the day. Isaiah had forced us to march round and round in circles for over an hour, kicking our legs high into the air as we sang the battle hymn of the revolution, a favourite song of Grandpa's.

'We're the End Time Army that's conquering hearts and minds and souls for the Lord! Lift up your Sword! Look to Heaven's Reward! We're the Revolution for Jesus and David our King!'

Every time we finished the song and collapsed on the floor, legs trembling, he barked at us: 'Get up, men. Again. Soooooldiers. March.'

It was ridiculous. I usually found some enjoyment in survival lessons. For one thing we were outdoors; secondly, I knew it was essential training and that any day I'd be putting the techniques into action. If I couldn't light a fire or know how to build a shelter, then how would I help my family survive the Tribulation? I had never been a top student, but in survival I began to excel. The marching, however, was pointless, and we knew it.

Just as we were walking back through the garden Vincent spotted one of the monkeys that made their home in the trees. The monkeys were really terrifying – very aggressive and vicious. From what we could work out there seemed to be two tribes. At night they would have gang fights where they had loud and protracted battles in a never-ending turf war. We would peer out the window to watch them pouncing onto one another's back, biting and scratching. Then others would appear from the trees, jumping on top until there was a jumble of monkey arms and legs kicking and hitting, all of them making the most dreadful noise – coughing, barking and screeching all at the same time. From the safety of the window we joked that even the Antichrist couldn't make such a din.

Vincent dug me in the ribs and pointed at a monkey, who was busy poking a finger in its ear. 'March, soldier. March,' he said, imitating Isaiah in a mock Irish accent. 'You have no discipline, soldier. Stop picking your ear and march.'

We both giggled. I looked away at the monkey for barely a second, but as I turned back Vincent was hanging in the air, his feet dangling like a ragdoll.

Isaiah had his thick hands either side of Vincent's neck, whose eyes were wide with fear. I looked up at Isaiah. His face was contorted with fury, but he said nothing. He just continued to lift Vincent, who was making awful choking sounds, higher in the air.

'Stop. Stop it, you are killing him,' I screamed. 'Put him down.'

Isaiah stared straight at me, not changing his grip on Vincent. Vincent's face was turning red and blotchy, the fear in his eyes now replaced by total panic.

'I said put my brother down!' The words spilled out with a force I didn't know I possessed.

Isaiah curled his lip in my direction. For a moment I thought he was going to kill me too. He dropped Vincent to the floor and walked into the house.

Vincent curled up, choking and gasping for breath. I lay with him, holding him and trying to calm him with my own breaths. Eventually his breathing slowed back to normal.

'I thought I was dead,' he said, his shoulders shaking with little sobs. 'My eyes went black.'

I sat him up and put my arm around him. We stayed there, not moving, until he felt ready to walk. I looked over at the monkey. It stared at us, wide-eyed and immobile. I think it too was stunned at what it had just witnessed. I swear it flashed Vincent a look of sympathy.

When we got back inside Isaiah was all smiles.

'Good work today, soldiers. Good work. Go get your shower. MCs' dinner at 1900 hours.'

Usually after survival training sessions Isaiah liked his 'crew' of MCs to have dinner together. 'A crew that fights together eats together,' he insisted. He could say that all he liked but I had no intention of fighting alongside Isaiah. When the time came my family would fight and die right next to each other. No way was I staying in his crew. And if he tried to stop me he would get one of my thunderbolts.

Isaiah's wife was Aunty Rebecca; she was as bonkers as her husband. Their sons Sean, Seamus and Seafra often got to choose the food we ate at crew dinners. Not that there was much choice – rice with lentils or rice with eggs.

They always asked their mother to make scrambled eggs. It was a total mystery to me, because Aunty Rebecca's scrambled eggs were a congealed, slimy mess. It was made worse by the fact all our food was bought in bulk, so very often the eggs were on the point of turning bad. It was like trying to eat putrid egg snot.

I did wonder if the boys only pretended to like her eggs because they knew we hated them so much. Aunty Rebecca took our refusal to eat as a personal insult. Wearing a hurt expression, she folded her arms and stood over us.

'Now I made these eggs for you naughty children and you don't even have the decency to enjoy it. Well, God be told, I never saw two more ungrateful wretches in all my life.'

Vincent and I tried everything we could think of to avoid eating them, stuffing our cheeks with the vile slime and spitting it out once we had been dismissed from the table. But that tactic meant putting the horrible stuff in your mouth in the first place. And Rebecca soon figured out what we were doing – her fat fingers would tug at the corner of our mouths and then we'd be forced to swallow the contents of our bulging cheeks.

Other times we would 'accidentally' spill our eggs on the floor – a self-defeating exercise because, if we were caught, whatever had fallen on the floor was shovelled back onto our plates by Aunty Rebecca, bits of grit, dirt and hair making it even more inedible.

The next time we came to the table, however, we had a plan.

Vincent and I smiled at Rebecca as we sat down and said grace.

'Thank you, Jesus. Lord, we pray that you bless this food that you have provided for us. Help us to be thankful for it and bless and keep all our family worldwide. Praise the Lord. Thank you, Jesus. We love you, Jesus.'

She watched us like a hawk as we picked up our spoons.

Isaiah was busy fussing over his boys. 'God sent me a vision last night, boys. Glorious it was.' Sean, Seamus and Seafra nodded as they slurped on their eggs.

Rebecca turned her attention to the conversation. She loved hearing Isaiah's revelations, particularly when it came to the wonderful plans God had ordained for her three boys.

'He told me, you boys, that he has plans for you in the End Time Army.' He paused, looking to see he had the full attention of his wife and sons.

This was the moment Vincent and I had been waiting for. While the others were listening to Isaiah's vision, we set about spooning the vile eggs into our pockets. Earlier that day we'd stolen some empty food bags from the pantry. Now these same bags lined our pockets, to prevent the eggs from oozing through our shorts.

'Jesus appeared in a blinding light, boys. Wonderful. What a thing to behold.'

I thought it was wonderful too. Isaiah was looking to heaven, recounting his vision, while Rebecca and the boys were fixated on him.

Vincent and I were growing in confidence and speed, emptying our plates as quickly and smoothly as we could, the warm weight on our hips growing with every scoop.

'Jesus told me you boys will be commanders at Armageddon and you will glorify Jesus and Father David with your courage and bravery!' Isaiah glowed with his revelation.

'Praise be to Jesus. That's amazing. What else did he say about my beautiful boys?' asked Rebecca, turning back to the onions she was frying.

'That is really amazing,' I chimed. 'Vincent and I have finished our dinner. Thank you, Aunty Rebecca. That was delicious.'

'Look, we ate it all,' added Vincent with an exaggerated enthusiasm I thought was sure to give the game away. I shot him a look.

'May we be excused?' I asked in my sweetest voice. 'I want to say some special prayers for my older brother in Victor Camp tonight.'

Aunty Rebecca eyed me suspiciously.

'Open your mouths. Both of you.'

Our jaws dropped in unison.

Rebecca seemed impressed by my new demure nature.

'You may leave the table. Please go straight to your dorm now and remain silent until you get there,' she said, almost happy.

I nodded with a sickly-sweet expression, doing my best impression of Honey, the mean girl who had bullied me in Bangkok.

As we walked down the corridor I felt like leaping into the air and whooping. We had put one over on the nasty old cow. We were learning the art of secret rebellion.

Mutiny at Tea

Summer turned into winter, Christmas came, and the New Year with it. Then summer came round again. There was still no sign of the End Time Tribulation and I still couldn't shoot thunderbolts.

A new sense of paranoia gripped the adults. Dad told me the Antichrist had invented a weapon, something called the Internet.

He was wreaking havoc with it. But it was also an important tool for us. A Shepherd came to install a big computer with a telephone and modem attached to it. We children were not allowed to touch it under any circumstances. If the phone on it rang three times and then hung up the adults would know it meant a message was coming through from HQ. The code was never to answer a phone until the fourth ring just in case. We also had a new warning code for when people went out witnessing. They were to drive up and down the street before coming in; if they saw a white sheet hanging from a bedroom window they knew it meant we had been attacked or raided by the government and they were to flee immediately.

Grandpa sent out a Mo letter informing us the prophecy hadn't come to pass because God had looked at us and decided we weren't ready. We had failed him. It would happen, but probably not for another three years. He told us we had better be sure we were ready next time. Isaiah was bitterly annoyed that his sons' chance of glory had been postponed. He became quieter and less frightening, brooding on his own failure to train his crew to the proper standards and thus displeasing God.

I had a sense something terrible was about to happen. The grown-ups began fasting and praying for days at a time.

They sat cross-legged, staring up to heaven as if in a trance or talking in tongues with sweat and tears pouring down their faces as they rocked back and forth.

One autumn morning I woke to the sound of wailing and howling. As we entered the dining hall for breakfast I saw my mother kissing a framed photograph.

'He was so beautiful,' she kept repeating. 'So beautiful. His eyes. Look at the light that shines. So beautiful. What a man. What a gentle spirit.'

She reverently passed the photo to Isaiah next to her as if it was a relic. He gazed adoringly at it, stroking his fingers across the glass. Rebecca took it against her heart, hugging it to her chest.

Some of the others were rolling around on the floor. It was pandemonium. Matt walked over to where Vincent and I stood. 'It's Grandpa,' he said in a flat voice. 'He's dead.'

I looked over at the weeping, wailing grown-ups. Rebecca had tears streaming down her red face. She shook her head in sorrow. 'The King is gone. Oh Lord. Jesus has taken him for an angel. Our King is gone. What will we do now?' She had the photo in her hand and held it up for us to see. 'Look, children, look at him. Here he is in all his God-given glory.'

I stared at the black and white image of an old man with a long grey beard. In all these years the only photocopied photos we'd seen had his face obscured by the cartoon lion's head. It had to be that way because the devil's soldiers would surely have murdered him if they had known what he looked like.

'See his beautiful face. Our beautiful King David,' my mother cried out. 'I knew he would be beautiful.'

But to me Grandpa had always been the drawn cartoon figure from my children's books – carrying his staff, a halo over his mane of long hair and a flowing robe. He was the all-powerful conquering hero of my childhood. The photo Rebecca held up was of an ordinary old man.

I wasn't really sad but it was impossible not to be swept up in such a public outpouring of grief. I threw myself onto the floor, wailing: 'Grandpa, Grandpa, Grandpa. Why did you leave us?'

Chapter 11

Walking with Buffaloes

Hypnotic incantations floated across the garden, hanging in the thick, hot air. Marching side by side, my parents circled the building as they chanted in joint prayer.

I sat cross-legged next to a rose bush, watching. I had baby Aimée in my arms. Guy and Vincent sat at my side. Guy, who had been so badly affected by my mother's forced long absence when he was two, was still particularly clingy with me, getting panicky and agitated if I disappeared from his sight for more than a few minutes.

He turned to me with puzzled look: 'What are Mommy and Daddy doing?'

'They are making our new house nice, sweetheart. It's called a Jericho march. Do you know the story in the Bible when Joshua and his army marched around the city of Jericho before they went into battle? Well, Daddy is doing that, but for our new home. Just stay quiet and watch him.'

Matt and Marc stood in a far corner of the garden, heads down in the type of private conversation the two of them seemed to have more and more these days.

Slowly, with a perfectly matched rhythm, Mom and Dad repeated their marches round and round the colonial-style green-roofed three-bedroom villa that was to be our new home. Mom suddenly drew a sharp intake of breath, as if she'd been hit with a large object. She fell writhing to the floor and started speaking in shrill tongues, but in two different voices, as though two people were having an argument.

Marc threw her a look of disdain.

She stood up, waving her arms in the air: 'Go, leave this place. Leave us. I cast you out.'

Dad followed her lead, also urging something to go.

After a few more laps and then going inside to repeat the process in each room, Dad came bounding out, grinning over to us. 'Welcome to your new home, everyone.'

I was 11. We had just moved country again, this time to Indonesia. We'd landed a few weeks earlier, having been told we were to be based in a large commune in Jakarta. I was not looking forward to being in a big group house again because memories of Bangkok were still all too raw.

But we arrived to the middle of chaos. Grandpa's death had led all sorts of people to start asking questions about The Family. Dad told us there had been lots of really mean articles in the newspapers saying bad things about him, calling him a madman and a drunk who liked to hurt children. I was upset on Grandpa's behalf. These people didn't even know him, so how could they say such things? My father said it was because the ones who were saying it were the crazy ones. The newspapers that wrote those things were in the western countries. The Antichrist controlled those countries and all the institutions in them, including newspapers.

But these stories had created such a problem for The Family that large communes were now deemed a security risk, attracting too much attention. All big houses were ordered to be broken up and their inhabitants dispersed into smaller groups, so they could blend in to the system more easily. Any material stored in communes that the outside world might think was bad – such as the Davidito book, *Heaven's Girl* books, Mene letters, Mo letters – were ordered to be burned in a project that the adults called 'the purge'.

Almost the moment we arrived, a Shepherd asked my dad to start helping him carry boxes of papers to a big bonfire they were building in the garden.

My parents were secretly furious. We'd just been moved out of a perfectly safe, small house in Malaysia. They'd dragged their kids to yet another new country, only to find there was nowhere for them to stay. On top of that my mom was pregnant again, with her eighth child.

Dad managed to secure a meeting with a senior Shepherd to plead our case. The man gave him some funds and told him to find himself a house for us all, but to make sure there was enough space in it to take another family or a few singles if needed. My father was nothing if not resourceful and after asking around the local area found us a villa that had stood empty for years. It had a certain charm but it definitely wasn't a palace.

We didn't have any furniture, beds or even mattresses. Mom asked if we could bring some spare things over from the commune but she was told that everything had already been allocated to others. When she questioned this she was told everything had been fairly divided according to need. It was clear that this was not the case. The senior inhabitants took the best furniture and anything valuable for themselves. That upset my mom. She was a pregnant woman with a large family. Surely that should have put us higher up the priority list?

She harked back to the early days of the group when a generous and giving hippy spirit filled the group, the days when someone would rather sleep on a cold floor than see a friend go without a sleeping bag. That ethos had long passed. In the end we managed to salvage a few battered pots and pans and some mattresses.

Despite Dad putting on a brave face we moved into our empty house with heavy hearts. The funds my father had been given covered the rent on the house but not any living costs. He was instructed to 'live by faith' and was given several boxes of pamphlets to sell on the streets. The normal rules applied – a percentage of what he made daily we could live on, and the rest was supposed to go back into the group coffers.

Every day he got up at dawn and pounded the streets, in the same way he'd done as a 17-year-old recruit back in Paris. But there was one big difference. Indonesia is a Muslim country. No one wanted to buy his leaflets, not even out of curiosity. People ignored him, pushed past him; others spat at him, calling him an infidel. If he was lucky a couple of old ladies might take pity on him, dropping him a few coins. He came back from witnessing exhausted, tired and depressed, and feeling like a terrible father for failing to bring enough money home to feed his hungry children.

An American uncle moved in with us. He was so creepy, and balding on top with a long ponytail at the back. He had sharp little teeth like a weasel. I hated the way he looked at me. Fortunately my mom noticed it too and did all she could to keep me out of his way, ensuring I was never left alone with him.

Life was definitely hard, in many ways harder than we'd ever known it. But for me there was a silver lining. For the first time in our lives we were a family unit. I shared a room with my siblings, and when we did have enough food for a meal we ate it together. No more Isaiah hitting me with a scrubbing brush, no more Aunty Rebecca force-feeding me eggs, no more twisted perverts like Clay and no more brutes like Ezekiel.

Or so we thought.

On a visit to the senior Shepherd's house to beg for more funds my dad was startled as someone called his name.

'Well, if it isn't me old mate Brother Moonlight. How are you doing? When did you get here?'

The voice was nasal, drawling.

My father turned to face him. 'Ezekiel.'

'Come on now, no need for that tone. Time to let bygones be bygones. I have forgiven you for your sins against me, Shepherd Moonlight. I know that messengers of evil poisoned your mind towards me. The Lord sure does test us, doesn't he?'

'So where did you go when you left Malaysia, Ezekiel? Straight here? I suppose I should have guessed.'

'Yes,' Ezekiel replied. 'The excommunication was taken to a higher level. No offence, brother, but you were wrong to do that. Your seniors thought so too once they'd heard the truth. They told me it was all hush-hush, to come here and start over. Away from mind-poisoning liars like you.'

My father shook his head in disbelief. In the past few weeks he'd arrived in a new country to find his family had nowhere to live, he'd been told to feed his kids by faith alone in a country with a radically different faith, and he'd seen a man he had thought had been excommunicated firmly still a member of The Family. In the past he'd had doubts, even wondered what it was all for. Now he felt blind fury.

For the first time since they had left France he was able to go home, stand in his kitchen and tell his wife exactly how he felt. Neither of them had to go share another's bed that night; no one could overhear them, no one was going to report on them. As he vented his rage she stood behind him massaging his shoulders. When he finished she cupped his cheeks in her hands and kissed him. 'Don't feed your anger. Find the victory, my love.'

He put his hands on her heavily pregnant belly. 'I'm sorry. I don't know what came over me. Maybe they were right to forgive Ezekiel if he repented. I don't know. I honestly don't know.'

She kissed the top of his head gently. 'Why don't we go pray? Children, come. I want us all to pray for Ezekiel and his family.'

We gathered in the kitchen, got down on our knees and did as she asked. As I prayed a vision of Clay floated into my mind. I flirted with the idea of telling them about the abuse. There was nothing to lose now and I was quite sure that they wouldn't accuse me of lying. But I let the thought go, deciding that telling them wouldn't change anything.

For a couple more months we bumbled along, hungry and worried about the future, but generally OK. Without the stress of other aunties and uncles monitoring our behaviour both my parents relaxed our usual discipline. One morning Mom took us completely by surprise. She was cooking a gratin for dinner but had run out of milk.

'Darlings, why don't you go fetch me some? Don't go far, just to that little shack two streets along, you know the one. Do not talk to anyone and come right back. Daddy will be home soon and this needs to be ready for him. Matt, you will be in charge. You make sure you all hold hands. OK?'

He nodded, his face a picture of excitement. She handed us a few coins and sent us on our way. It was astonishing. The only time any of us had been outside without adult supervision was back in Thailand when Matt and Marc had wandered outside to look at some birds. They were caught by an uncle and thrashed. I couldn't think of a single time I had gone out alone.

The four of us practically danced down the street. Fields of rice paddies surrounded the dirt road, and buffaloes wandered by, kicking clouds of dirt into the air with their hooves. Even when a man cycled past us wearing a pointed straw hat I didn't flinch. Our new-found freedom was more emboldening than scary. We turned left into the road, then right again and into a tiny local bazaar made up of a glass-fronted shop selling systemite medicines in little white boxes. Next to it was a wooden shack selling tins of food, milk powder, boxes of crisps and fresh fruit. Behind it, humming loudly, was a large refrigerator. I didn't like it. I pulled Vincent away, half expecting it to open and snatch us. Matt had taken on an air of seriousness as he pointed at the fridge and spoke to the man standing beside the shack. 'Fresh milk, please.'

I was in awe. Where did he learn to do that?

Matt fished in his pocket and handed the man all the coins. The man counted them, then handed Matt some back. Matt looked confused and handed them back over. The man gave them back, laughing as spoke in broken English: 'No. Too much. This change.'

Matt looked at the coins he'd been given, then at us, then back at the coins. 'No,' he muttered to himself, placing them back in his pocket. 'Come on, let's go home.'

I grabbed his hand, Vincent hanging onto mine. We'd barely got to the corner when Matt stopped, telling us to wait. He took the coins back out of his pocket, placed them in his palm and stared at them again. He looked at Marc questioningly.

Marc understood exactly: 'Yeah, why not? She won't know. Not if we don't tell her.'

We walked back to the stand, eyeing the goods in wonderment. By now it was obvious to Vincent and me that Matt intended to spend the change. My eyes lingered greedily on a packet of chewy sweets in a pink candy-striped wrapper.

Matt held out our booty to the man. He put the coins in his pocket, chuckling to himself, before handing over a little carton of yoghurt drink. He fished under his counter and pulled out a yellow plastic straw. 'Here. Take.'

Matt carefully opened it, put the straw inside and took a long sip. 'Oh yummy, this is gooood.'

Next he handed it to Marc. 'In age order, OK? No one be greedy and no one spill it. OK, Vincent? Be careful.'

One by one we took a careful sip, nodding and grinning at each other.

When we'd drained the carton of every last drop we walked home in a gleeful silence. As we neared the house Matt stopped us again.

'No one says anything. Right? This is our secret. Ours.'

We nodded at him reverentially, our new leader.

When we got home my dad was already there. He was sitting on the floor with his head in his hands. Mom was peeling potatoes, but she was also crying.

I ran over to my father, pushing myself onto his lap. 'Daddy. What's happened?'

He stared up at me with exhausted, dejected eyes. 'We are being deported, Natacha. We have to go to France.'

'France? I don't understand what you mean. Why do we have to go?'

His eyes met my mother's. They looked at each other for a very long time before he spoke: 'Because the system found us, that's why.'

Chapter 12

The Devil's Land

I've never been afraid of flying. When you are raised believing you will die in a glorious battle with the forces of Satan, a bumpy landing isn't much to be scared of. But I still squeezed the arm-rests as we touched down at Charles de Gaulle Airport in Paris. My father gave me a reassuring smile as we taxied across the tarmac.

'It'll be all right, Natacha.'

I wasn't so sure.

Paris looked like a catacomb from the air – a dark labyrinth filled with unknown dangers.

I should have been dead already. According to Grandpa, God felt we had failed to adequately serve him or demonstrate the necessary faith. But now Grandpa was dead and Mama Maria had taken over the leadership. Through God's mercy she told us the Apocalypse was rescheduled for 1996.

But here we were, heading straight into the belly of the Beast.

'Bonjour.'

My father handed our passports to the uniformed man behind the counter. I gripped my mother's hand and stared down at the floor.

'*Mademoiselle*?' I knew he was addressing me, but I didn't look up.

'*Mademoiselle*?' This time he said it with more force.

I raised my head and our gaze met. I tried not to let my fear show. As I stared into a pair of blue eyes the images of *Heaven's Girl* flashed through my mind. Would I soon die staring into eyes such as these?

'*Merci beaucoup*.'

He waved us through. My heart was pounding and I felt light headed.

A childish tittering roused me from my daze. My brothers were helping Dad collect our luggage. Our battered suitcases looked ready to spew their contents over the luggage carousel.

I turned my head towards the giggling. A girl of about my age was whispering into her mother's ear and pointing.

I shifted uncomfortably. 'Mommy, why is everyone staring at us?' I asked.

'Oh, Natacha, darling. Everyone is not staring at us.' She looked around. 'And if they were, it is because they are system people and they can see we are God's people. It is God's image shining in you that makes them stare so.'

'Do they want to hurt us?'

'No, my darling,' she continued, beginning to hit her stride. 'It is just that they have never seen the beauty of God's love made manifest in people such as us. And that is why we are here, remember – to share God's love with these lost souls before it is too late.'

I suddenly became very aware of my surroundings. Everything was shiny, clean, properly built and maintained. The people were neatly groomed in expensive-looking clothes.

Several of them were fat. Many of them smoked. Others looked bored, as if waiting for luggage at a gleaming airport in the Antichrist's stronghold was perfectly safe. Didn't they even know what danger they were in?

By contrast, we looked like refugees from a different planet. We were underweight, underdressed and under the impression that we were the normal ones – the ones, amidst all this material system wealth, who really knew what was going on.

Dad told us an uncle named Samuel was coming to pick us up. I was relieved to know we weren't expected to take a system bus. Samuel was waiting for us in the main concourse. He was tall and strongly built, with dark curly hair and deep blue eyes. He greeted us with a warm smile and hugged my parents vigorously. '*Bonjour, bonjour*, welcome to Paris.'

He and my father walked ahead, jabbering at one another in a language I didn't understand. Since moving to Thailand, American English had become my parents' chosen spoken language because that was the official language spoken in The Family. Mom had taught us a smattering of French vocabulary when we were alone with her, but English was my native tongue.

Samuel held open a huge metal-framed glass door and gestured us through it. I held back for a moment, not trusting him and wondering if it was a trap.

'Come on, *ma chérie*, hurry up,' Mom urged me on with a smile.

It was absolutely freezing. The first thing to hit me was the wind. An icy blast bit into my face, causing my eyes to screw up and water.

I think I fully expected outside to resemble a scene of nuclear devastation – flattened buildings, the stench of death, the hum of marching boots, voices of women screaming and children crying. Instead, when I managed to open my eyes I saw rows and rows of cars. Not like the battered cars in Thailand, Malaysia and Indonesia, but gleaming, shiny cars in so many different shapes I couldn't count. My father and Samuel were already pushing our trolley across some striped lines in the road, towards a field of hundreds more cars. I quickened my pace, desperate to get out of the wind.

Samuel walked in the direction of a large silver car with square lamps at the front. I heard Matt mumble, 'Oh wow, please let it be that one.'

Instead Samuel opened the door of the battered black Renault estate next to it. Matt looked crestfallen. Even I felt a bit cheated too, wondering how we'd all fit in. My father rode up front. Me, Mom – who carried baby Andy in her arms – and Aimée were in the back seat with Matt and Marc. Vincent and Guy squeezed into the boot space with our luggage. Driving through Paris was horrible. I was still tense and frightened, wondering if we might get stopped at a checkpoint or if a bomb might fall, but from what I could see it didn't look like any bombs had fallen. Everything was still standing, people walked along the pathways, the roads were wide and well kept. It didn't look there was a war going on at all.

To me Paris looked unnaturally clean. At the very least I had expected to see people being murdered in the streets, babies thrown from prams, drunken violence and drug use – all the depravities of the 'system' I had heard so much about but experienced so little of.

I was really confused but I thought it best not to admit it. I didn't trust this Uncle Samuel and thought he might be a spy.

After an hour or so we left the city streets behind, the lush French countryside beckoning us on. I began to relax as my mother sang a hymn to pass the journey.

'*Amazing Grace, how sweet the sound, that saved a wretch like me. I once was lost but now am found, was blind, but now I see.*'

We travelled east, to what Samuel told us was the Champagne region. The landscape in Champagne was like green corduroy, stitched from the grapes that Samuel explained made the region world famous. I don't think an adult had ever taken the time to explain a journey to us before. Usually when we went witnessing no one even bothered to tell us the name of the city, but Samuel pointed out landmarks and buildings. I was beginning to think he might be OK after all.

My brothers and I made a game of staring down the rows of grapes as we flashed by. Each row offered a different view from the next. It was as if each one was a single frame of film and we were watching some strange movie. It made me dizzy and giggly and happy.

'Here we are, everyone!' Samuel declared as we drove into a little town up a steep winding hill. I couldn't quite believe it. It was like a fairytale, with little timber-framed cottages clinging to the side of the hills. When we pulled up outside our new home my eyes nearly popped out of my head.

The house was the most romantic thing I had ever seen, with rustic beams and low ceilings. It even had a log fire, which Samuel lit for us. We all immediately huddled around it, shivering. Our clothes were completely inadequate for the French climate.

Samuel took my mom and me into the kitchen to give us a tour. He opened the cupboards, which to her delight were full of pans, plates and bowls. He'd even been thoughtful enough to buy a box of groceries – bread, milk, biscuits, pasta and vegetables – ahead of our arrival. I could have kissed him.

Before we left Indonesia the senior Shepherd had come to see us and given my father enough money to last three months, telling my father that was the maximum he'd been authorised to give us. Very quickly we realised it wasn't going to buy much at all. Even if we were careful it would probably only stretch to a few weeks. My father decided the best way to make some money fast was either by 'parking' – which meant standing in supermarket car parks and trying to sell literature – or by performing music. I found parking excruciatingly embarrassing; playing music made much more sense to me because performing was what we did best.

We walked to the edge of town, where Samuel had told my father there was a large supermarket. It had a huge red neon sign saying Carrefour, a word I had never seen before. We took a spot by the exit, my dad started to strum the guitar and we sang our hearts out.

A man pushed his trolley outside, packed high with crates of beer. He walked past us, sneering: 'Crazies.'

He was the first of many.

One elderly woman stopped and stared at my mother, barely able or willing to hide her distaste. 'Bloody gypsies,' she hissed at us, before spinning on her heel and striding across the car park.

A few people took pity on us – mostly the poorer agricultural workers. Perhaps knowing poverty makes one look more kindly upon those who suffer from it.

The cold was making the little ones ill. Vincent developed a horrible rasping cough and baby Andy couldn't stop crying.

My father promised my mother he would fix it somehow. Later he and I walked through the town as he stopped passers-by asking if they knew of any places offering free clothing or other charity items. Most people walked past us or shook their heads blankly. A man in a thick woollen coat stopped. As he talked to my dad all I could think about was how warm it would feel to be wrapped in that coat. He gave my dad a lifeline. 'There's a donated clothing centre run by the Catholics. It's mostly for homeless folks, but I reckon they'll let you go there. What are you? Some kind of missionaries?'

'Yes, we are,' said my father proudly. 'We are here to warn people of the last days of the world before the second coming of Christ.'

'Maybe you should think twice about telling them that!' joked the man as he wrote the address down on a piece of paper and gave it to my dad.

'Daddy.' I tugged at his arm. 'Catholics have lost their way to heaven. We can't go to that place.'

He gave a sad little shrug. 'I think … we need to take whatever we are offered. You children need to stay warm. That is the most important thing for me right now. Jesus will understand.'

The next day we found the place, a large hall packed with rows of musty-smelling second-hand clothing. Women in headscarves with children as scruffy as us pulled at the racks, barging each other out of the way to fill up their baskets with stuff.

My mother had gone pale. And that's when I caught a look on her face. Not regret, but perhaps the acknowledgement that her life might have been so very different.

My father and the boys had already started piling into a rack of woollen men's sweaters. I followed their lead and started grasping at a rail of women's clothes. I pulled out a cardigan. It was so soft and warm it felt like touching a hug.

'Well, Mom, what do you think?' I asked in a tone that sought approval.

She picked it up with her fingers, examining it for holes, then turned it inside out to read the label. 'Cashmere,' she enthused. 'Not bad work, Natacha.' And with that, off she went, elbowing rivals aside with the best of them as she fought to find the best clothes for her family.

After that our life became completely dependent on charity. Every day my father would take either Matt or Marc, who were 15 and 14 respectively, and comb the nearby towns in search of organisations that might be able to help us with either food or money.

They went everywhere on foot, even in driving rain or heavy snow.

One cold evening Dad arrived home particularly late and, as was so often the case, empty-handed. Marc had been with him. When the pair of them had left in the morning it was already raining, but by late afternoon a thick icy fog had settled in. Marc had only one pair of flimsy leather shoes with a hole in the sole.

As he stumbled through the door I rushed over to help take off his oversized tweed coat. 'My feet, they are sooooo cold.'

He couldn't wiggle his toes and I struggled to get his shoes off. I pulled off his wet socks; his feet were swollen and blue.

I fussed over him, making him sit in front of the fire and bringing him a bowl of hot water to put his toes in. He almost cried with relief. 'Oh, thank you so much, that's better. Much better.'

Once both he and my father were settled, I began to prepare the family meal. Mom was busy upstairs feeding baby Andy. There wasn't really much to do: boil some water and put a packet of spaghetti in it – it was all we had to eat.

I searched through the cupboards trying to find a tomato or a few bits of left-over cheese I could grate over it to make it nicer. But just as I was feeling gloomy about our situation something occurred to me. As poor as we were, badly dressed, hungry and cold, we faced these problems together, as a family. Just us. I carried in the food and plonked it down with a beaming smile.

After a few months, once we began getting government welfare benefits, our poverty eased. My parents had spent their lives deriding all governments as evil, yet now the government 'system' was the only thing saving their kids from starvation.

'It won't be for long,' my father asserted, assuring us that the Apocalypse was still on track. It was just that the situation in France wasn't quite as bad as Grandpa had feared. He warned us that this didn't mean we could relax; we still had to be on our guard at all times.

In order to qualify for the benefits, the local government officials insisted we children had to attend intensive French language lessons.

It was my first real encounter with other children outside of The Family. I was struck by their smart school uniforms, which made me nervous, because uniforms always meant soldiers or other 'system' dangers, but I was also a little bit jealous. Our second-hand clothes marked us out as different. I liked the girls' skirts and their smart blazers, and I was in awe of the confident way they spoke to each other. They looked so grown up, and although I felt like an outsider I was beginning to glimpse that perhaps we, not them, were the ones out of step.

I think we would have been badly bullied were it not for Matt and Marc's popularity. Matt had my mother's good looks, with a long dark ponytail and big brown eyes. He was a confident, funny joker, a natural leader of the pack. Despite this also being his first time mixing with outside children he had no problem making friends, somehow making it into the cool kids' gang. I suspect they found his difference and background a bit edgy, much in the same way my mother had found my father's background attractive when they first met. Marc was quieter than Matt, a brooding, sensitive type. Looks-wise he took after my father: he was tall with dark eyes, olive skin and thick black hair. He was a ladykiller.

Mom was thrilled when Joe graduated from the Teen training and flew out to France to join us. Sadly, to me he had become a stranger. The brother I had known was gone … He didn't play or joke with us; he rarely even spoke unless spoken to first.

Joe only stayed a couple of months before deciding to return to Thailand and to a girlfriend he had left behind there.

As the year drew to a close we were still desperately poor, but we'd managed to kit ourselves out with hats, scarves, jackets and woollies, so we were warm at least. I had seen pictures of snow before, most memorably the snow-capped mountains in our weekly screening of *The Sound of Music*, but seeing it thick on the branches of the pine trees and carpeting the garden was magical.

That year we spent our first Christmas together as a family. On Christmas Eve I was so excited I could hardly sleep, the first time in my life being happy had kept me awake. When morning came I rushed in to wake up the younger ones.

'Aimée, wake up. It's Christmas. Come on, sleepy-head. Guy, time to get out of bed. Come on. Let's go build a snowman.'

Like giddy lambs we tumbled down the stairs, to find my parents already standing in the kitchen sipping hot coffee.

I looked at my father hopefully. 'Daddy, please can we go out and play before we say our prayers? Please.'

I really didn't expect him to say yes. Back in the communes I'd have got the fly-swat for even daring to ask.

He beamed a big fat indulgent smile: 'Go on, get out there. And make sure that snowman has a hat on or he'll get cold!'

Vincent and Aimée cheered. Mom secured their knitted bonnets under their chins and made them put on their mittens.

'This is going to be the best Christmas ever,' Vincent declared.

And it was. After lunch of a roast chicken, vegetables and potatoes – not much, but a feast to us – we walked through the town as the snow fell in perfect round flakes. In the market square there was an outdoor carol service. We took our places alongside the systemites. They didn't seem so different to us – children rosy cheeked and bundled up in winter coats, their moms and dads relaxed and happily holding hands. Thoughts of death, destruction and Armageddon didn't even occur.

When the service ended we walked back home, happy and giddy as we scooped up snowballs to throw at each other.

That was the best day of my life.

Chapter 13

Stirrings

I eyed the glass suspiciously and sniffed it. Its smell was sweet, with hints of nutmeg and vanilla.

'Go on. It won't poison you.' Marc laughed.

I wasn't so sure. Eggnog – even alcohol-free eggnog – seemed to imply it had eggs in it, and I didn't like eggs.

I took a tiny sip. It was thick and cloying, and its texture was just a bit too close to Aunty Rebecca's horrible scrambled eggs.

'Urgh!'

It made my head shake from side to side in a spasm of revulsion.

Marc laughed again. 'Not for you, then?'

'No,' I said, regaining my composure. I was suddenly mindful of all the other teenagers around me. 'Maybe next time.'

I was reasonably confident there would be a next time. I had just hit my teens, 13. The end of the world was still nigh; supposedly it would begin any time that year. All that mattered to me was that it didn't start this week because Marc and I were at a Family-run teen camp in the Belgian Ardennes. It was the first time I had been away from home and I was super-excited. Tonight was dance night.

Stirrings

A Latin disco number, produced by The Family's own music and meaning team, played at full volume. We weren't allowed to listen to any music that hadn't been either made by our own musicians or approved by the leadership.

The prettiest older girls were holding court in the middle of the dance floor. Shaking their hips suggestively and flicking their long hair, they would twirl towards the boys. The atmosphere was so sexually charged it felt electric. This wasn't the type of gross flirting we saw the adults do before they had sex. This was different. This was thrilling to be a part of, even though I felt on the fringes, not really knowing what to do.

The camp days were spent listening to lectures about how to fight the devil's temptations, or hearing testimonies from adults who had led depraved, drug-fuelled lives before being saved by The Family. We were at the age at which The Family thought we might start rebelling, so the camp was organised to remind us of our role as 'witnesses' to the end of time and to help us be more spiritually mature. But it was also a lot of fun. Growing up I had never played sports before; our PE lessons consisted of swimming, playing games like hide-and-seek or tag, or doing aerobics to cult-made exercise videos. At camp they had real games like football and volleyball every afternoon. I didn't play because I didn't want to look even less cool than I already did.

Instead I joined the organised walks on trails through the pine forests. I was going through my poetic, melancholic phase, convinced I was the deepest and most misunderstood girl in the world.

Some of the older boys were camping on the lawn outside the lodge we had rented for the week. This provided plenty of opportunity for couples to get together. It was obvious that the camp leaders knew what was going on, but they didn't mind. They actively encouraged it.

I was very nervous and shy. I had just got my first period, which only added to my adolescent insecurity. Thank goodness Marc didn't mind me hanging around with him. Matt was at the camp too, but he was busy doing his own thing and hitting on girls. He didn't want gawky little sister tagging along and cramping his style.

A euro-techno pop song came on, all synthesised beats and cheesy words of love. Caleb was on the other side of the dimly lit room effortlessly talking to a group of girls. I felt a pang of jealousy – they were close enough to stare into his beautiful brown eyes. I had to make do with admiring his athletic physique. He was gorgeous, funny, popular – and out of my league.

He looked over in my direction and waved. I had half started to wave back when I realised his wave was meant for Marc. What an idiot. I could feel myself blushing deeply as he made his way over to us.

'Hey, man,' he said to Marc.

His eyes really were beautiful. And his shoulders were even broader up close. It was like staring at a teenage Richard Gere.

'Hey, Caleb. How's it going?'

'Hi …' I said weakly, running out of words.

'Cool, talking to the chicks, dancing. You? Knocking back a few 'nogs, I see.' He nodded at my brother's glass.

Marc laughed. I smiled, not really following their conversation, but staring in adoration instead.

'That German kid drank his body weight in eggnog – then thought it would be a good idea to show some of the girls how many press-ups he could do. Last time I saw him he was throwing up in the garden.'

'Smooth. Yeah, the girls all love that stuff!'

More laughter.

'Actually,' Caleb went on, 'I came over to ask a question. I wondered if I might have a dance with your little sister.'

I couldn't believe my ears. Marc began to answer, but I didn't give him the chance.

'Yes. I mean, yes, you may.' I grinned at Marc. I sensed Marc had set this up. He knew I had a crush on Caleb, but I didn't care. I held out my arm, inviting Caleb to escort me the dance floor. I felt like a princess with my handsome prince at my side.

Just as we got to the middle of the room the song changed to a slow power ballad. Everyone started to slow dance. I was blushing again – I could feel the heat on my cheeks. My mind was blank and I couldn't think of a single thing to say, so when he held out his arms I just put my head on his chest and drank in his scent.

After the dance he walked me to my room like a proper gentleman. There was no moment of embarrassment or teenage fumbling. Instead it was as if we had an unspoken bond – something that didn't need words to be communicated. As he walked back down the hall I just waved goodnight, which he returned with a flash of his gorgeous smile.

This was more special to me than anything. Sex was banned for the under-16s, but lots of campers were managing to do it. If we'd really wanted to we could have snuck away and had some sneaky sex in his tent. But for Caleb to walk me to my room and not so much as kiss me made the evening feel like there was something magical going on.

It was a feeling that stayed with me when I woke the next day. A thick mist had carpeted the pine forest valleys overnight, so that only the mountain top poked through. It was a wonderful sight and I felt like God had planned it as my own special surprise – a sort of beautiful morning to a beautiful night.

'So? Spill.'

It was my new friend Jeanette – she was blonde, beautiful and an insatiable gossip. We'd made friends the first day. I was over the moon that she liked me because she was so pretty and the envy of every other girl at camp. She came from an aristocratic French family and exuded a sort of natural grace with the delicate features of a porcelain doll, a little bit like I imagined my mother had looked at the same age. But she was also very timid and shy, which is probably why she felt at ease with me.

'Oh, gossip. What's going on?'

Another new friend, Sienna, trotted towards us, pulling back her dark hair. She and I had become very close over the last few days, but in this instance I wasn't so pleased to see her – she was Caleb's sister.

'Somebody was dancing with your brother Caleb last night,' blurted Jeanette.

'Oh, that's old news. I thought you had something juicy.'

I was so relieved Sienna wasn't being strange about it.

'In fact,' Sienna went on, 'I spoke to the man himself just before, and he seemed rather pleased with himself.'

'Ooohhhhhhh …'

I knew where Jeanette was going and cut her off.

'You can calm down. Nothing happened.'

This just fuelled Jeanette's curiosity.

'Really? I thought you liked him.'

'I do. I really do. Sorry, Sienna.' I touched her arm in one of those 'I know it's a bit gross talking about your brother like this' ways. 'I do like him. But nothing happened, I promise. He walked me to my room and we said goodnight. It wasn't weird. It was just … nice.'

'Urgh. The "N" word.' Jeanette really couldn't help herself at moments like this. 'He must really like yooouuuu,' she said, sending her voice into a high pitch that climbed with her knowing eyebrows.

When the final day of camp came round everybody was a bit demob happy. We only had one lecture – a kind of round-up of the week's lessons on fighting the lures of Satan.

Afterwards I was sitting on the grass with the girls when Caleb sauntered over.

'Hi, Natacha.'

Jeanette pulled an 'Oooohhhhh' face silently behind his back.

'Hi, Caleb. You want to take a walk?' I surprised myself with my boldness, but I was desperate to escape Jeanette's antics.

'Sure.'

We went down through the woods to the lake. I didn't really know what for, but I was just happy to be alone with him before we had to go our separate ways.

He took my hand in his as we walked along the shore.

'It's so beautiful here,' I said, taking in the stunning view one last time.

'I know what else is beautiful.'

I turned my head back to Caleb, catching his soft lips with mine. My head spun with the sheer joy of it and for a moment

I thought I might topple into the lake. It made me cling to him even tighter. I could have stayed there for ever, except some other kids came crunching along the shoreline.

We pulled our heads apart with a little smile.

'I guess this is goodbye, Natacha. For now.'

On the drive home I couldn't stop thinking about that kiss. I ran my finger over my lips where his had touched mine, and hid a little smile.

I was still smiling when I walked into our kitchen. My father was sitting at the dining table poring over documents.

'Hi, Daddy.' I ran over to him and kissed him on the cheek. 'What you doing?'

He ran his hand through his hair and sighed, slouching in the chair.

'It's my mother's last will and testament. She died some years ago. I never knew. My sister just told me.'

'What?' I had never met the woman, yet somehow I instantly felt her loss. For the first time ever I thought about our other relatives. Who were they? Did they know we existed? Did they believe in Jesus like us? I had no idea what they looked like, where they lived or what kind of jobs they did. They were my blood relatives but I knew nothing about them. That realisation saddened me.

Then over dinner he made a shock announcement – we were going to pioneer a new country where The Family wasn't known. The place we were going was called Réunion.

I didn't really know what to think. My mother looked perfectly happy about it. She patted her belly where her ninth baby was growing inside. 'And you would like to be born into an exciting new mission, wouldn't you, little one?'

Matt, Marc, Vincent and I looked at each other a little bit stunned. Since moving to France my parents had been pretty much cast adrift by The Family, especially financially. If they'd wanted we could have easily left for good. The last thing we expected was for them to drag us half way round the world to be missionaries again.

Only Vincent could manage the obvious question.

'Where's Réunion, Daddy?'

'It's a little island near Madagascar. It's a colony so they speak French, and we can get welfare there so we won't starve either. They don't know God and there are no Family members, so we will be true pioneers for the Lord. Sounds great, doesn't it?'

I had very mixed feelings as we boarded the plane at Charles de Gaulle Airport. Arriving here two and a half years ago I had been a terrified child, expecting to be murdered the moment we landed. France had been unexpectedly kind, allowing us a glimpse of normality – school and a normal family life, two things I wasn't ready to leave behind.

But as the plane descended over Réunion I felt like I was in a dream. Its rugged volcanic peaks and unspoilt coastline were matched by the inhabitants, such as the witch doctor we nearly ran over in our car as he prepared an offering of freshly slaughtered chicken, rum and fruit in the middle of the road. I'll never forget leaving the airport and seeing a road sign warning of waterfalls ahead. We all laughed at the silliness of it, but then as we turned the next bend, there it was – a waterfall right in the middle of the road.

Friendly locals warned us from the start not to be fooled into a false sense of security by the undeniable beauty of the island. We were told to watch out for gangs of desperately poor teenagers roaming the streets, drinking and looking for opportunities to enrich themselves at someone else's expense. When my dad heard this he immediately slapped a ban on my going anywhere without his or a brother's supervision. The black magic, or *gris gris*, that Réunion's cultural life ran on was spoken of in hushed tones in our house.

Our new home was a small concrete house surrounded by sugar-cane fields from where my father would conduct his missionary work, heading out daily to surrounding villages to spread the message. I was relieved that we were the first ones there and didn't have to move into an established commune, as I'd had my fill of bullying children and cruel surrogate parents. My father home schooled me, something he did with a great deal of impatience. When not taking my lessons, most of my time was dedicated to helping run the house or look after my younger siblings. It was very lonely for a 14-year-old girl.

I started to get sleepless nights again, often waking up after a bad dream to find my sheets soaked in sweat. I constantly felt anxious and sad, unable to work out exactly why. It was as if I was walking around with a great big heavy rock on my head.

Marc and I had become much closer since hanging out at youth camp. I felt that of all my brothers he was the one who understood me best because we were similar types. He could tell I was going stir crazy with the sense of confinement so he persuaded my father to let him chaperone me to the beach, a short bus ride away. We spent the afternoon confiding in each other about how sad we were. Marc told me he wasn't even sure he believed in any of our teachings any more. He'd spoken to some other boys at camp who'd had similar doubts. He was seriously thinking about leaving the group, but he had no idea how.

Chapter 14
A New Wine

We were all were gathered in our living room ready for Word Time. I loved the fact that these days we got to do it as a family, which made it all seem so much more intimate and fun. Sometimes we chanted, other times we meditated in silence, waiting for our individual prophecies from Jesus. My faith was extremely strong and I took my prayers seriously.

'I want to share something with you. Mama Maria has sent us a new revelation,' my father said, shuffling a thick sheaf of papers. Revelations from Maria were coming in fast these days as she attempted to assert her leadership with a new set of guidance and rules, something she referred to as 'the new wine'.

He started to read: 'Come in unto me – let us be one! Let us love! Let us lie in each other's arms. Kiss me, caress me, fuck me and love me, fill me to the full! Like you say, "Hold me!" Like you say, "I love you! I want you! I desire you! Come lie with me! Come fill me."'

I cringed with embarrassment. The last thing any 15-year-old girl wants is her father saying the word 'fuck'.

I got the sense he wasn't any more comfortable than I was, but he carried on; 'So the Lord's prophecy is clear. Listen to this.' He read more from the letter, explaining these were Jesus's direct words given to Maria.

'Do not be ashamed or afraid to speak these precious words of love to Me, for they are as special incense, special prayers that come up before Me, that fill My halls with a special perfume, a perfume of love and of lovemaking! It excites Me! It thrills Me! It makes Me want to give to you, and give and give some more, and again and again! As the thrust of a man upon a woman in lovemaking, so I want to give and give and fill you with My seeds! For when I smell this perfume in the halls of Heaven, I look upon you with great love and with great care and with great excitement, and I want to fill you to overflowing like none other can fill you! These things of the flesh are only a mere speck of the love that I have for you! But I give you the touches and the words and the feelings of the flesh and the sensations and the orgasms, the kiss upon kiss, the breast to breast, the being held, so that you will understand how I am with you.

'So love Me and be not ashamed! Do not be afraid to say that you want Me. Do not be afraid to say that you want Me to fuck you and to love you and to kiss you, to hold you. For it is in these words that you convey the feeling of your heart. Yes, I want praise and adoration, I want words of thanksgiving, but they that love Me most understand that I also want words of caresses and words of wooing and words of endearment.'

I couldn't believe what I was hearing. When Jesus spoke to me it was usually to show me the way through a problem. He never said anything like this. I knew I loved Jesus; I loved him with all my heart and soul. But making out like I wanted to have sex with him? It sounded ridiculous.

I glanced over at my brothers and sister. Marc's ears were glowing red, a sure sign he was embarrassed too. Matt was throwing my father one of his murderous expressions. Vincent was trying not to giggle.

My mother, however, was on her knees in prayer, her face down. Occasionally her head bobbed up and down in agreement. 'Oh Jesus, sweet Jesus.'

I begged Jesus not to let her break into any dirty talk. That was more than I could have coped with. Dad droned on in a similar fashion for another hour. Thankfully he didn't make us discuss it at the end. I don't think he could have coped with that either. Alone upstairs later, Marc and I sat on my bed talking in horrified whispers.

'Would you really do that? Could you?'

'No way,' he replied. 'I'm a guy. Sorry, but I just don't get how I am supposed to pretend to be a woman. I couldn't do that if I tried.'

The letter from Maria explained that when men and boys talked dirty to Jesus they should do so as a woman and that they should consider themselves his bride. This was because Grandpa had hated gays. Being a homosexual was something that got a person excommunicated. Jesus was most definitely not gay so the only way a man could love Jesus sexually was by becoming a 'woman in a spiritual sense'.

To Marc it was beyond offensive. 'I mean, come on. How the hell am I meant to do that? It's kind of perverse, don't you think? I don't even know what it means. Even if I did want to suck Jesus's seed, which I do not by the way …' At that I collapsed in giggles.

He shot me a look of admonishment. 'I repeat … I said I do not. But even if they were standing over me making me do it, I have no idea what a woman even does when she masturbates. I mean, I know what she *does*, but what does she *think*? Oh man, this is messing my head up.'

At dinner that night I found it hard to even look at my father. Were he and Mom going to do this later that night?

The thought grossed me out, so I took it from my mind. I don't think I'd ever really considered my parents' sex life before. Of course sex was an everyday thing for me. I'd seen so much of it happen growing up, but they were my parents. I think every kid in the world gets freaked out thinking about their own parents doing it. So thinking about them doing it with Jesus … was just really, really weird.

My mother was busy talking about Mama Maria, extolling her virtues as leader. 'I did wonder at first if she'd be able to cope with it. And I did think the charter of responsibilities and rights might have been a step too far. You know, I think she and King David lived in their ivory tower for so long I feared they were losing touch. But she seems to be leading well. She's a good manager.'

The 'charter' my mother referred to had been announced in February 1995, not long before we left Indonesia. It was a key part of the 'new wine', setting out a code of rules for all members of The Family which stated that the secondary responsibility of a Family member was to believe that Father David and Mama Maria were God's true and only End Time prophets. My parents had been unusually reticent about it, openly questioning to each other whether this was a sign the power had gone to her head.

Dad certainly seemed less sure as he discussed what we'd read today. 'So this "new wine". It certainly shines a light on bridal theology. I'm not sure that's something I understood before. It's challenging, but if I am getting the guidance in the right way she is saying that He truly becomes us, becomes our flesh.'

It would turn out a great many other second-generation members, especially the boys, shared my and Marc's revulsion. Many of them were already struggling with the discipline, the poverty and the lack of freedom. This new doctrine sent a shockwave through the group, prompting a number of second-generation children to leave.

In a bid to stem the tide of growing unease, specific guidance was then issued for teens. 'We have prayerfully gone over the material to make sure that it is suitable for your needs … Also, we don't want to be guilty of giving you junior teens reading material that would be offensive or not legally permissible for people your age from the System's point of view. We want to give you as much Word as we can, without going too far or causing any legal problems for The Family. We need to try to stay within the law.'

As it goes on it clearly reveals how she feared the doctrine might be perceived in the outside world: 'By worldly standards, it is not very proper for a Christian to say "dong" and "cunt", as those words are considered dirty slang words, but the Lord instructs us that if He chooses to use them, then they are clean, and we shouldn't be offended or disgusted or turned off by them. However, just as you don't make "fuck" a part of your normal everyday vocabulary, so you shouldn't with these words either, especially not to outsiders!'

And, as always, there was the subtle reminder that none of this was being 'forced' on us, it was our 'choice': 'Unless the Lord speaks to your heart personally and lays on your heart the burden to do it, you don't have to feel as if you must masturbate. All of this is a very private matter, something between you and the Lord. If you want to love Jesus while masturbating, that's up to you.'

But Mama Maria saw any negative questioning as a direct threat to her new leadership and took further steps to control the damage. She dismissed any critics of the 'new wine' as renegades when she published her next letter.

My father took the opportunity to share her words once again at the family dinner table. 'I hesitate to spend too much time talking about those few who had such a difficult time that they chose to leave The Family. But it's important that you understand that most of the ones who left over the "Loving Jesus" revelation were those who had been weak and "sitting on the fence" for quite a while.'

'So, according to her, these troubles had already been foretold. But it's really a blessing.' Dad continued to read aloud:

'Earlier prophecies have indicated that there would be a purging of our ranks. Do you recall in "Mama's Love Story, Part 3! – King Peter!" there was a prophecy about how the Lord would "rattle the foundations" of your faith? And He explained that the reason for such "rattling" is to test, purge and purify The Family.'

'But Dad, it's just weird.'

My father looked puzzled for a moment.

'Ah, well. You're not alone there, Marc. It's a spiritual concept, not merely a physical one. Even Mama Maria has had to challenge her own mindset. Listen to this, point 72:

'This uncomfortable feeling is a result of something that isn't of the Lord, and the devil uses that feeling of awkwardness to try to prevent us from talking about it or doing it, or to try to get us to stop talking about it or doing it. But if we'll go right ahead and do it, in spite of feeling uncomfortable, the more we do it, the more comfortable we will get with it. The more we talk openly about it, the more quickly it will become just a natural part of our life.

'So you see, Marc,' said my father, 'the more you do it, the more you'll get used to it. But like I said, I believe this is a spiritual thing that we are each meant to approach in our own way.'

'But Dad, the same could be said of anything. You could argue I could drink poison and get used to it after a while.'

My father was getting frustrated. 'Marc, stop being ridiculous.'

'But Marc does have a point, doesn't he, Dad?' I said, trying to help Marc out.

'If our benchmark for testing new revelations is simply to ask "Will we get used to them in time?", then the answer is almost certainly "yes",' replied my father. 'In which case Marc is right – this family has proved time and again that almost anything can be endured, even enjoyed.'

I cocked an eyebrow at Marc.

'Who says we are to test them, Natacha?'

My mother had taken an interest now.

'Revelations are to test us, we are not to test them. We are to "get the victory" in all things. That's what King David taught, and that's what the Lord wants of us.'

'Indeed.' My father was beaming. 'Well said, my darling. You are always the truest of all disciples.'

He leaned towards my mother and kissed her on the cheek.

'Well, maybe I don't want to be a disciple.'

My father's good mood vanished.

'What did you just say, Marc?'

'Maybe I want to leave,' he muttered, unsure of himself now.

'And do what, Marc? Go where? Become a drug addict living on the streets of some God-forsaken Western country, enslaved by the system and fighting with the Philistines for whatever scraps the Antichrist or his followers throw you. Is that what you want, Marc?'

My mother tried to calm the situation, pleading with Marc.

'Son, you know God loves you. And God wants you here, among his people as part of The Family. Don't throw that precious gift of his love away. He's done everything for us. You have been chosen to be part of his elite army. How can you deny such a high calling?'

'Yeah …' The fight had all but left Marc now. 'I guess …'

'Good,' my father said firmly, turning to all of us. 'We'll have no more of this nonsense now.'

Later that night Marc came into the room I shared with Vincent and Aimée. He sat on the end of my bed and told me he couldn't see a way forward any more. The 'Loving Jesus' guidance was only part of the reason he was determined to leave. He just couldn't see eye to eye with my parents any more.

'But Marc, where will you go? How will you manage?'

He looked crestfallen at the question. 'I'll live on faith, I guess. Isn't that what we've always done?' He let out a bitter, wry little laugh.

Marc didn't know anything about how the system operated; none of us did. In France we'd learned that system people kept their money in banks but we didn't know what an account was or how to open one. We didn't know what a CV was or how people applied for jobs. We didn't know about electricity bills, how to buy a train ticket, how to book an appointment with a doctor – none of the things children who had grown up in normal households knew. We weren't normal. That much we definitely knew to be true by now.

'I do know one thing though, Natacha. When I make enough money I'll come back and get you. I want you out of The Family too. The men in this group aren't good enough for you.'

I got out of bed and hugged him. 'I know you will. You'll be OK, Marc. You'll do it.'

Chapter 15

Changing Tides

Matt took a long, exaggerated drag on the cigarette, then handed it to Caleb, who nodded appreciatively. 'Nice, man. Gauloise. The philosopher's smoke.'

Caleb puffed in what he imagined was a sophisticated way and passed it to his sister Sienna. She gave it a tentative little suck before hurriedly handing it to me. I was determined to look like I knew what I was doing in front of Caleb. I copied what he'd done, taking a long puff and inhaling it deep into my lungs.

I spluttered so hard I was almost sick. It was disgusting. Matt rolled his eyes at me. Caleb laughed. 'You nutter. Not so hard the first time. Here, let me show you.' He took the cigarette between his fingers and gently placed it back in my mouth. 'OK, gently. Just a little bit, not too much … that's it.'

I really didn't want another go but Caleb's face was inches from mine. He smelt so good.

I took a little puff and only spluttered a little bit this time. 'Good girl,' he said proudly.

I beamed.

Skulking around, hiding from our parents and doing forbidden things like smoking and drinking had become pretty normal for us. Two months earlier, completely out of the blue, Caleb and Sienna's parents had written to mine to say they were also inspired to move to Réunion. I had been ecstatic at the prospect of seeing him again. Thankfully he felt the same way. Almost from day one we started seeing each other. Matt and Marc were brilliant, covering for me so I could meet him. Matt started to date Sienna. They made a great couple. She was the perfect foil to his wit. She was a little bit quieter than him but she was also extremely funny, and they made each other laugh constantly. Together with Marc and Eman, another teenage boy who lived with Caleb and Sienna's parents, the four of us had now become a little gang of six naughty rebels. Life had suddenly become much more fun.

Sienna had a slumber party at her house. All of us were there. As everyone else slept Caleb reached over and kissed me.

'Let's do it. Here. I want to do it so badly with you. Don't you?'

Actually I didn't. I was terrified. But I didn't know how to say no.

Caleb and I were both virgins, and, despite having watched people have sex all through our childhoods, when it came to doing it ourselves we were both pretty useless. It wasn't helped by the fear of one of my brothers waking up while we were in the middle of it. When it was over I wondered what all the fuss was about and was certainly in no hurry to try it again.

Unfortunately my mom suspected something had gone on and tricked me into telling her the truth by pretending to already know. She immediately told my dad, whose liberal sexual attitudes failed him when it came to the thought of his precious little girl doing it. He hit the roof and banned me from seeing Caleb without a brother as chaperone. Secretly it was a relief because it meant I couldn't be pressured into more sex.

Matt was our gang leader. He was fearless. One of his favourite tricks was stealing money from my father's witnessing funds to buy local bootleg beer or cigarettes. He had to be careful not to take so much as to get detected, so sometimes the stolen booty only got us one bottle of beer to share between six. But for us it wasn't about getting drunk, it was about the illicit pleasure of breaking the rules. It could have been stolen jam for all we cared. The point was that it was illicit, taken from right under my father's unsuspecting nose.

We hung on Matt's every word. He and Caleb, his deputy, were wisecracking, cool guys. Vincent tried to follow us everywhere but Matt usually brushed him off, telling him he was still too young and more likely to get us caught.

My parents suspected Matt was the instigator of a lot of trouble but didn't really want to believe their son was becoming such a 'backslider'. As much as possible they tried to stick their heads in the sand. Caleb and Sienna's parents knew what was going on and my father was upset at a rift that developed with the couple, who had until then been their good friends. He made his displeasure known, constantly sniping at Matt. One evening, over dinner, he accused Matt of talking with his mouth full. It was a tiny thing, but it escalated:

'I was not talking, Dad. I was chewing. You know, that thing you do to food. Like this.' Matt made exaggerated chewing movements, followed by a little sneer.

Dad was in no mood for it. 'Don't talk back to me, Matthew. I am trying to teach you good manners. Goodness knows we have tried all these years, and where has it got us?'

Matt shot a look. 'And what is *that* supposed to mean?'

'Do you really need me to explain? Shut up and eat your dinner.' Dad slammed his knife into his plate, trying to control his anger.

'Shut up? Oh yeah, that's your answer to everything, isn't it? Tell us to shut up. And teaching us manners? Is *that* what you think you did?'

The rest of us, including Mom, stared nervously at our plates. We were getting used to these angry exchanges between them. Our policy was generally to stay quiet and not inflame either of them further.

My father carefully put down his knife and fork and raised his elbows onto the table, staring Matt squarely in the face. 'Grow up. You are about to become a father yourself. Show some maturity for once in your life.'

Matt couldn't resist the last word: 'Oh yeah, Dad, I am going to be a way better father than you.'

At that my dad was up and out of his chair and halfway across the table, his eyes blazing.

'Marcel, calm down.' My mother was on her feet, one hand on her husband's arm. 'Matt, go to your room and stay there, please. You are a rude young man and this is not the example I expect you to set to the younger children. Apologise to your father immediately.'

'Sorry.' Matt slouched out of the room, the muscle in his cheek twitching.

My father sat back down and we finished our meal in uncomfortable silence.

The halcyon days of our little teen gang were about to come to an end. Sienna had fallen pregnant and she and Matt moved into their own house. They horrified both sets of parents with the shocking news that their newborn baby would not be brought up with our faith because both of them were quitting The Family.

Caleb and Sienna's parents had been offered the chance to 'pioneer' Madagascar in the way my parents had done on Réunion, that is, to set up a brand new commune and take The Family's message to a new place where it didn't already have a presence. That was seen as a very holy thing to do and something that earned them a lot of praise from the leadership.

Caleb, who had just turned 17, bravely told them he wasn't going either, because he was following his sister in quitting the cult. He took the decision to move back to France where he said he would find a job and send for me when he could. Kindly Uncle Samuel agreed he could stay with him for a few weeks until he got himself sorted.

When Caleb came to tell me his news I felt like I had been punched in the chest, a sensation made worse by the fact he didn't seem half as upset as I was. 'At least it gets me off this boring island,' was his reaction.

How could he say that? I didn't know how I was going to live without him.

The night before he left we sneaked away into our favourite little hiding place in some sugar-cane fields. As I lay with my head on his chest he stroked my hair and promised me he would write to me every day.

After he left I was so depressed I could barely move. I wasn't allowed the luxury of moping. Life was still a relentless routine of helping my mother with the younger children and keeping the house clean. I had no one to have fun with any more. Impending parenthood had made Matt and Sienna all grown-up and no fun any longer. Vincent had taken to wandering off on his own as often as he could, and Marc was in a constant bad mood.

I think I was so absorbed with my own misery that it had stopped occurring to me how unhappy Marc might be too. When he told me we needed to go for a walk outside so he could tell me his news I was completely unprepared.

'I'm going. Next week. I'm leaving The Family.'

It shouldn't have been such a shock. He and I had discussed it for months, even more so since Matt had renounced the cult. I knew he hated his life and had no belief left in the way we'd been raised. But I also knew that we didn't know any other way of life. Deep down I don't think I really thought he'd have the courage to do it. He told me he had been in contact with two other second-generation members who had left – friends he'd met at the teen camp in Belgium. Having been ridiculed as 'backsliders' by Mama Maria and cut off by their families, ex-members began looking to each other for support. Informal flat-sharing clusters sprang up in Paris and London. Marc had been invited by his friends to join one in London.

My parents were deeply disappointed. They gave him the usual warnings about how he faced a lifetime of sin – drugs, drink and all the temptations the devil might throw at him.

'You are turning your back on God and no good can come from this,' my father told him angrily. 'If you think you are grown-up enough to make this worldly decision then you go ahead, but don't think for a second you can expect me and your mother to help you out when it all goes wrong. And mark my words it will go wrong. There is nothing to be gained from a life on the outside. Nothing.'

The day Marc flew to London was the worst of my life. Still reeling from Caleb's departure, I was now losing my confidant, the brother I trusted the most.

Over the next few weeks Caleb's letters started to get more and more intermittent, until they stopped arriving altogether.

I asked Sienna to find out why. He'd moved on but not even bothered to tell me. He was living with Jeanette, my old friend from camp.

On my sixteenth birthday I woke up feeling like an old lady. Instead of looking to a future full of promise and adventure, I felt like life had already passed me by. I stopped eating, making excuses as I picked at my food. I imagined myself as a pitiful heroine wasting away from a broken heart.

I very nearly got my wish. I got peritonitis and was rushed into the local hospital for emergency treatment. I spent a week there staring miserably at the ceiling. To make it worse I also developed septicaemia, a serious blood infection, and had to have intravenous antibiotics to stop it poisoning the rest of my organs. I lay there staring at the florescent light above my bed, sinking deeper and deeper into depression.

My parents weren't quite sure what to do with me, but they figured they had better try something to cheer me up or risk another child leaving the faith. They'd recently got back in touch with Leah. She'd found out where they were and had written to say she was happily married and living in Mauritius with her husband, Edward, who was from there.

She had three children with him, and Thérèse, now 15, was living with them. She and Edward were both still devout members of The Family.

I was thrilled to hear any news of Thérèse, and to cheer me up my father asked Leah if I could go to visit them. I felt very loved and special that he'd arranged this. I knew the money for the ferry crossing was very hard to come by. It was the first time I'd travelled by boat and I was violently sick on the way there. High waves caused the boat to lurch from side to side and there was nowhere to sit as every wooden bench was crammed with people nursing brightly wrapped parcels of luggage, crates of food, even live goats. I still wasn't well after my stint in hospital and the journey totally took it out of me. But as we docked I was in high spirits, craning my neck for a glimpse of my second mother and my little sis. As I scanned the faces lining the harbour it occurred to me for the first time that I might not recognise them.

As I stepped off the gangplank a bulky, swarthy-looking man approached me. He stuck out his hand. 'Natacha?'

'Yes. That's me.'

'I'm Uncle Edward. Come on.'

With that he turned on his heel, gesturing for me to follow. He didn't offer to help me with my bags; he didn't say, 'Pleased to meet you.' He didn't even crack a smile.

The rest of the trip was a disaster, played out in a similar way. Leah, although delighted to see me, was under Edward's control. I got the distinct impression she was regretting ever asking me to come.

But the saddest thing of all was Thérèse. Physically she still reminded me of the little girl waving goodbye from the minibus window. She had the same dark ringlets and intense blue eyes. But she was really quiet and reserved, almost afraid of her own shadow.

I had hoped for some teenage bonding, but it wasn't to be. When I told her my brothers and I smoked and drank alcohol I thought she might be impressed, but she was horrified. I tried to talk to her about my own growing doubts about The Family but she shushed me. Instead of flying by, my week with them dragged unbearably. I arrived home with a groundswell of anger in my belly towards The Family and her father. She was his but he'd let her be taken away from him. What had poor little Thérèse done to deserve that?

Marc rang often. When he called, my parents made a little bit of small talk but they rarely asked for the details of his life. They didn't want to hear it. My mother usually reminded him to say his prayers or told him to 'get the victory'.

When she passed the handset over to me he confided he was struggling to cope with life. The shared flat was squalid and overcrowded and his friends partied a lot, smoking dope and spending most of their evenings getting hammered. He was incredibly lonely. He wanted to find a girlfriend but he said system women found him too intense. If he tried to tell a girl about his past they ran a mile.

'It's not like I thought it would be, Natacha. It's so much harder.'

I had nothing to say that would make it better. He was living a life and facing pressures I couldn't begin to understand. Usually I just tried to offer platitudes, telling him I was proud of him and that he'd work it out.

He had to.

Because if Marc failed in the outside world, then what hope of escape was there for me?

Chapter 16

Happy New End Time

'Ten, nine, eight …' The countdown had already begun. All around us fireworks exploded to a backdrop of music and laughing voices.

I looked over at my father. He was nervously checking the sky for signs of Armageddon.

My mother reached over and gripped my hand.

'… five, four …'

I took a deep breath. We could be dead in seconds.

'… three, two …'

This was it. The End Time was nigh. Everything was about to be plunged into a blackout. Chaos would reign.

'Happy New Year!' The night sky lit up in a myriad of colour and noise as champagne corks popped.

It was the year 2000, the start of a new millennium and a worldwide party.

My family stood in our garden staring at each other, wondering when? If?

After a few minutes the fireworks began to subside. The lights were still on in the house. There was no screaming or panic, only the sound of 'systemites' having the party of their lives.

Vincent laughed out loud. 'Sooo, looks like we're still alive? Happy New Year to you all.'

We laughed with him, although I don't think Dad was entirely relaxed yet.

Mama Maria had warned us to expect Armageddon at the stroke of midnight. She sent word that all followers should be ready and prepared for the great battle.

Once a warning like that would have sent me into panic and had me practising my thunderbolts. But that was before the endless drills and training for two other Armageddon prophecies that had failed to come to pass, back in 1993 and then again in 1996. This time I didn't really believe it. Throughout December I had helped my parents carefully stockpile our food supplies, candles and survival kits, but I had a nagging feeling none of it would be needed. My parents didn't voice any doubts to me but I had a sense they weren't as fully on board with it as they once might have been either.

My father was still looking at the sky, unsure if the fireworks were actually bombs in disguise. I thought I caught a glimpse of sadness in his eyes. Part of him wanted the prophecy to be true. He had spent his life waiting for the time to be God's soldier and martyr. At that very moment he should have been striding through the air, protecting his family, waiting for his battle orders, saving lives, saving the world.

Instead he picked up baby Chris (who had been born a couple of months after we arrived in Réunion) and went and sat on a garden chair, lost in his own thoughts.

My mother sat next to Vincent and me as we pretended to relax and enjoy the atmosphere like normal people. None of us dared voice the words that echoed around our heads like a clanging bell. The leadership had got it wrong. Again.

When I woke up the next morning with the sun streaming through my window I burst out laughing. The world, despite the global hangover, was still as it was. Three times now they had told me it would end. Three times it hadn't. I knew now beyond all certainty that The Family had been making it all up.

I swore to myself that I would not listen to their lies any longer. I was determined to join Marc and live my life my way.

Mama Maria had begun to loosen the rules in a bid to stem the flow of people leaving. The strict sobriety rules had been relaxed. My parents now enjoyed a glass of red wine over dinner. She'd also ended the ban on members contacting biological families, owning property or inheriting wealth. That turned out to have some wonderful consequences for us. My father's friend Silas had inherited millions from his parents. Silas had known my father since the very early years of the group. I knew he came from a fabulously wealthy family and I had never understood why he'd chosen to live as a missionary in such abject poverty. But, despite his newfound wealth he clearly still had the generous hippy values. He invested in a couple of properties on Réunion and gave us one to live in rent-free.

It was without doubt the most stunning house I had ever seen, with a huge kidney-shaped pool in the garden. For the first time in my life I had the luxury of a bedroom to myself. But overall I was still an unhappy teenager and very much a prisoner. It felt like all I did was clean up after others and look after the babies. I was like a housewife. My mother was pregnant yet again and not able to do much. I resented the burden falling to me and wondered why she insisted on constantly having children when she was clearly exhausted and struggling to cope. Andy was four and a half and Chris two and a half. Between them she was run ragged.

In early May she gave birth to twin boys Louis and Laurent. They were adorable and I loved them on sight, but as I looked at their peaceful sleeping faces all I could see was more work for me.

The twins were bad sleepers. As soon as one drifted off the other one woke up, or if one started crying the other followed suit. I got into a routine of taking them out for a walk in the pram before bedtime to try to get them off. It had the added bonus of helping me escape for a while.

I was lost in my own thoughts when I felt someone looking at me. 'What lovely children! Are they yours?'

I looked up into the most stunning aquamarine eyes I had ever seen. They were set into the face of a Greek god. He introduced himself as Jean-Yves, a local island boy. He was half Creole and half French.

After hastily explaining that they weren't mine but were my little brothers, Jean-Yves asked if he could walk with me.

Before long I was jumping out of my bedroom window every night to meet him. At first we hung out on the streets, snatching kisses wherever we could. But then he introduced me to a man called Bear. Bear lived alone in his shack and was happy to let kids come and hang out there, drinking and smoking weed. At first I didn't want to go, assuming Bear had some kind of ulterior motive. But for once I was wrong. He was just a lonely man who enjoyed the company and genuinely believed that if kids were going to do that, they should do it somewhere safe and not on the crime-ridden streets. We spent many fun hours hanging at his shack where Bear always made a point of listening to my problems. I hated leaving but I knew I had to get back at a reasonable time to avoid detection. Jean-Yves would walk me to the house and watch until I had hoisted myself over the fence, crept across the front garden and climbed into my window.

My days were intolerable. I was desperate to be with Jean-Yves. If I wasn't changing nappies or feeding babies I was out witnessing with my father. He had a battered old van now and would drive it around the island's villages, trying to sell cult propaganda to disinterested shopkeepers. Witnessing wasn't the fun day out it had been as a child. These days it was pure humiliation and anger as I stood there listening to my father spout a theology I believed in less and less every day.

My life cheered up a bit when we took in a rescue dog called Gypsy. When she arrived she was filthy, with matted brown fur and covered with fleas. She was a mess, but I was instantly in love. She became my best friend and confidante, a kind of canine replacement for my far-away brother.

In early summer Marc came back from London for a short visit. Things were extremely tense between him and my parents. They pointedly didn't ask him about his systemite lifestyle. They didn't want to hear about any of the bad things he'd got up to, which I could understand, but he clearly had so many problems and worries that he needed to download. The strain on his face was clear. But they didn't give him the opportunity to talk. I was really angry with them for this. OK, so they hadn't cut him completely adrift like Mama Maria had ordered the parents of 'ungrateful backsliders' to do, but they were not exactly offering much practical or emotional support either. He made it clear that he was in dire straits financially and barely able to make ends meet, but my parents told him they weren't giving him a penny, reminding Marc they had warned him this would be the case. He was the one who had chosen to leave and now he had to face the consequences of his actions.

Matt and Sienna had just gone back to France, to the relative safety of Uncle Samuel's house in Paris. Samuel was still a member of the cult but he was unusual in that he didn't judge and had a real sympathy for the young people who were leaving and trying to make their own way in the world.

I felt wretched, like I was losing everyone I loved. I blamed my parents for forcing them away.

'I hate Mom and Dad. This is their fault,' I complained to Marc on his last night. 'If they didn't let Mama Maria tell them what to do all the time we'd all be happy.'

Marc shook his head sadly. 'No, we wouldn't, Natacha. We lost that chance years ago. This is just how it is. You tell me when you are ready to leave and I will fly back here and get you. OK? Just say the word and I will be there.' He threw me a wink. 'Don't leave it too long, though, eh? They might get you married off. Or you might run away with your Creole lover.'

I'd confided in him all about Jean-Yves. 'Ha, ha. I'm not that stupid. I don't want to get stuck on this island all my life.'

The next morning when he left for the airport I had an awful sense of foreboding. I couldn't shake it off for the rest of the day. It was like a black mist – just this horrible gut-wrenching feeling something awful was about to happen.

But I wasn't the only one suffering.

It hit Vincent very hard. He was 14 now and still the fragile, difficult boy he'd always been. He was rarely to be seen, usually hanging out in his secret weed-smoking den in a little hollow between the rocks at the bottom of the garden. I worried he was smoking a bit too much, but when I tried to challenge him about it he fobbed me off. There was no way I was going to report him to my parents, so I didn't share my fears with them. Besides, my selfish head was too full of Jean-Yves and finding new ways to sneak out and meet him to worry about Vincent.

I wish I had, because three weeks later Vincent tried to suffocate himself with a plastic bag. He panicked when he ran out of breath, and yanked it off.

It was the first of two more suicide attempts, each one worse than the next. The second time he overdosed on aspirin. He told my mother what he'd done and fortunately started to vomit them up. He looked and felt truly wretched afterwards and promised me sincerely he'd never try anything so stupid again.

He seemed to be a bit calmer and happier after that, but he was lulling us into a false sense of security. In his own mind he was determined to do it again.

We were all sitting in the living room when he walked in, dazed and shaking. He started to speak but then started convulsing and fell to the floor.

We all ran to him at once. His eyes were rolling in the back of his head and he was making an awful groaning noise. The children were crying and screaming. I remembered some basic first aid from survival training and got him into the recovery position, checking his airwaves to make sure he didn't choke on his own vomit. Everything was a blur as Dad lifted him into the back seat of the car. I got in beside him and we drove to hospital. Dad's knuckles were white, gripping the steering wheel as he sped around hairpin bends. I was absolutely terrified we wouldn't make it in time.

Vincent was rushed into emergency surgery to have his stomach pumped. He admitted to the doctors he had drunk a bottle of white spirit. Fortunately the hospital was new and had good facilities. As we sat in the waiting room my dad put his head in his hands and wept.

When Vincent came round, he refused to come home. In the only way he could show how serious he was about not doing so to my parents, he asked the doctors to admit him as a mental health in-patient instead. He stayed there for the next six months, insisting it was preferable to home.

Vincent's pain only served to make me hate my parents even more than I already did. They didn't have the faintest idea why he was so unhappy. 'What would make him do that?' my mother asked me the night we came back from the hospital. I wanted to throttle her.

They couldn't see what damage the cult upbringing had done to their children. I began to think of it as wilful ignorance on their part and lost all respect for them.

After a night of drinking at Bear's house with Jean-Yves, I was climbing back into my window, my shoes in my hand, when the light came on. My father stood there looking at me. 'You are drunk. So this is what you do at night? When your mother told me I hadn't wanted to believe it. But look at you, a filthy little drunk who cavorts with local boys. I am so unbelievably disappointed in you, Natacha. Of all my kids, I expected better from you.'

I was in no mood for a lecture. 'So what if I am, Dad? What are you going to do about it? Beat me? Go on then.'

He didn't flinch, just stared at me with a look that said disgust, disappointment and failure all rolled into one. 'Go to bed. This stops. Tonight. I'll be damned if I'll see another backslider in my household.'

At his departing back I shouted, 'I don't care what you think. Don't you get it? I don't *care*.'

I fell into bed and cried myself to sleep. My father ignored me for days, refusing to acknowledge my presence. I had always been such a daddy's girl, but now I honestly did not give a monkey's what he thought of me.

Because I couldn't sneak out any more, Jean-Yves dumped me. That hurt me much more than my dad's silent treatment.

Chapter 17

A Door Opens

I was 17 and a half. The half mattered a great deal because it meant six critical months away from being 18 – the age when I was going to leave home. I absolutely detested my parents these days. It took all my effort to be polite to them. I loved my younger siblings dearly, but I was seething with resentment that my life offered nothing more than feeding and changing them.

Then out of the blue my escape route revealed itself, or rather himself.

I was buying groceries at the store when I found myself staring at a strongly muscled back in front of me. I didn't really pay much attention but he'd obviously spotted me because after I'd paid for my shopping he offered to carry my bags. He introduced himself as Thomas, a 34-year-old chef from the French city of Lyon, who worked in one of the local hotels. He was gorgeous, with a mop of unruly blond hair and a cheeky smile.

As we said goodbye he asked if he could meet me on Saturday evening at a popular bar. It was the first time I had ever been asked out on a proper date. I didn't hesitate in saying yes.

On Saturday evening I spent ages in my room getting ready, then walked downstairs into the living room where my parents were both sitting reading. My mother looked up. 'Why are you dressed up?'

My father turned to her. 'Because she thinks she's going out somewhere, but she's not. Go back to your room please, Natacha.'

I gave him a fake smile, more of a lip curl. 'No. I'm going out. And that's because I am an adult now so you cannot stop me. I don't know what time I will be back. *Au revoir*.'

With that I turned on my heels, slamming the door as I went. I was a little shaky when I got outside, expecting to hear a 'Naaaataaaachha, get yourself back in here *now*.' But there was nothing.

Thomas was charming, funny, and seemed quite the epitome of sophistication. I couldn't really believe my luck and never questioned why it was that a man so much older and apparently successful was interested in a 17-year-old girl who knew nothing.

He told me he loved me on our third date. I said I loved him too. I did – with an all-consuming passion that blew me away. I thought back to Caleb and Jean-Yves and wondered what I ever saw in them. They were little boys; Thomas was a man. And I'd already decided he was going to be my saviour.

One week short of my eighteenth birthday I walked into my parents' bedroom and gave them the speech I had been rehearsing in my head for months.

I told them I was leaving them, leaving The Family and moving in with Thomas. It didn't come as much of a surprise. They both just looked at me in silence as I spoke. When I had finished my dad simply said, 'We won't stop you.'

In some ways I wished they had, or at least tried to talk it through with me. They didn't ask me any questions about how I felt about Thomas, how he felt about me, what our future plans were – none of the things any sensible parent would want to discuss with a teenage daughter moving in with her boyfriend for the first time. Just like they were with Marc, they simply didn't want to know about anything we did outside The Family, so deep was their disappointment. It was as if I had turned to a life of crime. I thought I had been a good daughter. I had always helped my mother run the house and take care of my siblings. But it was as if any good I had done had been wiped away simply because I did not want to stay in the cult – their cult. I was their child. Wasn't that enough to make them love me unconditionally? That it clearly wasn't was what hurt me the most.

Inside I was a quivering mess. I was doing my best to convince myself and everyone around me I was grown up enough to be able to make such a big decision. But even I knew I was kidding myself. In reality I was a little girl playing at being an adult. I had no idea how relationships were supposed to work. I thought that doing all the cooking and cleaning, like my mother had done, was probably a good start. Thomas lapped that up.

Sex wasn't brilliant. I still didn't really enjoy it. Thomas had an almost pornographic sex drive and wanted to do it two or three times a day. I had been raised to believe a woman's duty was to service a man whenever and however he liked it, so it never occurred to me to refuse him.

Thomas drove over to pick me up the day I moved in. He looked uncomfortable as he shook hands with my father and kissed my mother briskly on the cheek. 'I'll look after her,' he mumbled. Their faces were like stone. He couldn't wait to get out of there, quickly throwing my bags in the back and urging me to get in. 'Let's go then, Natacha. Shall we?'

Since coming home from hospital Vincent hadn't made any more suicide attempts, but he was certainly no cheerier. I hugged him and kissed the little children one by one. They were all lined up on the driveway, waiting to see me go. Vincent looked truly furious with me. 'What am I supposed to do now?' he asked.

'I'm sorry. But I'll come and get you whenever you're ready.' I used the same line Marc had given me. I hoped I said it with the confidence he had said it to me, but I doubted I'd pulled it off in quite the same way. Vincent certainly didn't look convinced, and with good reason. We were both really worried about Marc. A couple of days before he had called home and confided he was in big trouble.

He'd recently got a job with a car rental company as a night security guard. He got drunk on shift with a colleague, taking a company Mercedes for a spin, and ended up crashing it into a wall. He was so naïve he didn't even realise it was a criminal offence until his boss told him he had informed the police. Of course he was fired too.

He was terrified. He didn't believe the police were Antichrist soldiers as we once used to, but he still had a fear of uniformed authority. He had no idea what kind of punishment he'd get and if he'd go to jail or not. But the thought that he might do so spun him into panic. On the phone he told me he planned to flee to France and stay with Matt.

'I hate London anyway. France is easier to live in. It makes sense, right? I can get a job there, can't I?' His voice was almost pleading, desperate for reassurance. But this was all completely out of my frame of reference. I had no idea what to tell him to do for the best. I thought running away was risky but I couldn't bear the thought of him locked up in a 'system' prison either. He begged me not to tell my father, not that I had any intention of doing so anyway. Dad would just say he'd told him so, that life on the outside always led to crime.

'Just do what you think is best. You'll work it out, you always do,' I said somewhat lamely as I hung up.

My first night as Thomas's official live-in girlfriend was bliss. He had cooked me a dinner of fish and salad, washed down with champagne and chocolate mousse. It was all so surreal and, to me, so deliciously classy. I imagined we'd live like this for ever, curled up in our little love nest. Tipsy and blissed out, I fell asleep.

It must have been around 5 a.m. when the phone rang. Thomas woke, reaching over to answer it with a grunt. 'It's for you,' he said, handing me the receiver.

'For me? Who?'

'I don't know. I was asleep.' He looked at me angrily. 'Who the hell wants to talk to you at this time?'

I had no idea. For a minute I thought it might be my father calling to demand I come home. 'Hello. It's very late. Who is this?'

Matt's voice was crackly and distant: 'Natacha, I can't reach Mom or Dad. Where are they? It's urgent.'

'Matt? What? Are you in France?'

He spoke impatiently. 'Yes, of course France. I need to talk to Mom or Dad. Where are they?'

Thomas stared at me, his face a picture of tired irritation. I was embarrassed and, completely unfairly, annoyed with

Matt for waking Thomas up and disturbing our new-found sanctuary. 'Well? Who is it?'

'Matt,' I mouthed, putting my hand over the receiver. 'Sorry. I'll get rid of him.'

Thomas grunted again and rolled back over. 'Please tell him not to make a habit of calling here.'

I spoke into the phone: 'Matt, you are not to call me here. This is my home with Thomas now. OK? I live with Thomas now. Night, night.'

Without waiting for a reply I hung up the call.

Half an hour later it rang again. Thomas started to stir. I was scared at what he might say. Quick as a flash I leapt across his back to reach it first: 'Matt, I told you …'

Matt cut me off mid-sentence. 'Shut up and listen to me. Marc is dead.'

The world went blank.

Chapter 18

A Caged Bird

The days that followed the news were a whirlwind of pain.

We learned that Marc had arrived in the city of La Rochelle the day before he died. He'd gone to meet up with Eman, our old friend from Réunion who had quit the group at the same time as Caleb. He had promised to help Marc find a job.

Later they met up with some of Eman's friends. They went to a bar, where they drank, then on to someone's house to get high. Then they went for a drive. We don't know why. One of Eman's friends was driving, going too fast and showing off. On a country road he lost control in black ice and wrapped the car around a tree. He survived, but both Marc and Eman were killed. Marc was alive for ten minutes but died just before an ambulance reached the scene. It was the tiniest comfort to know a French farmer had witnessed the crash and held Marc in his arms as he passed.

Matt was distraught. Joe flew out from Bangkok to join him. I assumed my parents and I would be on the next flight out to France. But no.

My father gave me the news. 'Sorry, Natacha, we don't have the money for you to go. And even if we did, who will look after the children? Your mother and I have to go alone.' The words were like a body blow.

I got right up to his face, almost spitting with fury. 'I *need* to go. Don't you get that? Why should you be there and not me? I need to go. Who was there for him for the last few years when he struggled all alone in London?'

My dad's face contorted with rage and grief. 'Shut up. How dare you say that in front of your mother. She has lost her son, you selfish girl.'

My pleading came to nothing. I had no choice but to leave Thomas and move back home for a week to play mother to my youngest siblings. I don't know how I got through the next few days or how I managed to take care of the kids because I was nothing more than a tearful ball of tightly wound fury. I blamed everyone for Marc's death, but mostly I blamed God. Marc had been an outcast from the moment he decided to leave the cult. He had been so very alone in the world. How could that be fair or right or just or Godly? How could God allow him to die before he had even had a chance to live?

For the next year I barely left Thomas's apartment. We lived in a small flat near the beach. It was just fifteen minutes' drive from my parents' house but I only visited once every couple of months, and even then I stayed for as short a visit as I could get away with.

Since Marc's death I had been in a very dark place. After two short-lived attempts at getting a job, first as a barmaid and then a waitress (both jobs only lasted one evening), I gave up even trying. I was so messed up that just stepping outside the front door sent me spinning into a panic.

I suspect my fear was something Thomas knew he could take advantage of so he could keep me in check.

Thomas was big into tantric sex, so our love-making sessions would go on for hours, always with candles and New Age music. Most of the time I was there physically but not mentally. I would bend my body obediently into the next strange position he ordered me into from the copy of the *Kama Sutra* he kept by the bed. Sex was a difficult thing for me and I often felt scared or tense without knowing why. I also sometimes had flashbacks about Clay. But I obediently did whatever Thomas asked me to do even when I hated it. It's hard to describe the feeling of being pressured to do something sexually that makes you feel sick, and hating yourself for it even more because you agreed to do it.

If I had been older and wiser I might have realised that a man his age was probably only attracted to a dysfunctional teenager like me for one thing – sex.

Thomas had quite a big group of friends, all in their mid to late thirties like he was. Because I was odd and socially inadequate I did not fit in one bit. Most of them barely bothered to talk to me. His ex-girlfriend was part of the same group and he seemed to take a nasty pleasure in flirting with her in front of me to try to make me jealous.

I recall one party in particular. It was a poolside barbecue at one of his friends' houses. Thomas was doing his usual flirting with his ex while I sat in a corner alone. I remember at one point late in the evening, when they were all drunk, he and the ex were playfully laughing and groping each other and he pushed her into the pool. The ladder was near where I was and I will never forget the way she looked at me as she climbed out of the pool with her curly dark hair and wet shirt clinging to her breasts. She smirked at me with a victorious look on her face. To me she looked like the embodimemt of a she-devil.

I felt totally wretched and had a bad headache to boot. I asked Thomas if we could go home but he said no and told me to go and lie down in a room inside until he was ready to leave. I didn't think I had the choice to demand we go so I did as I was told, while he continued cavorting in the pool with his ex.

When we finally got home in the early hours of the morning he started to talk about her, telling me about the things she used to do to him in bed. I told him it was upsetting me but he made me listen as he went on and on. He said if I really loved him I would try to be as good at sex as she was, beginning now. I still felt poorly and was holding back tears at his attitude but I made love to him that night all the same because he was all I had in the world and I was desperate not to lose him.

When Thomas suggested we leave Réunion I heartily agreed. He thought Thailand, so popular with backpackers and full of busy hotels and restaurants, was a good place to find work. I readily agreed. For the first few weeks it was bliss. Thomas even proposed to me, getting down on one knee in a bar and presenting me with a cute little diamond ring.

We managed six months before we completely ran out of money. I had assumed he'd take care of that side of things. I didn't really have any idea how anything worked on the outside and I had been brought up to expect a man to look after me. We had been staying in a cheap hotel but hadn't paid for the past two nights. The manager was threatening to throw us out onto the streets.

A Caged Bird

With my heart in my mouth I put my last few coins into the payphone and dialled home.

'*Bonjour*.' It was my father.

'Dad, it's me. I can't talk for long. I'm so sorry, Dad, and I wouldn't ask if I wasn't desperate, but I need some money. It's really urgent. We need to …'

'No.'

I hadn't even got to explain why. 'But Dad, you don't understand. We haven't got anywhere …'

'I said no. You made your bed, Natacha. Now lie in it.'

With that he hung up on me. I don't think I could have hated him more.

Next Thomas rang his mother. He had better luck. She offered to buy us two flights to her home in Lyon the next day. France, the country of my grief, had definitely not been on my agenda. Nor had living with Thomas's mother, whom I'd never met. But it was our only option.

No one came to meet us at the airport, which I thought was an ominous sign. Fortunately Thomas had a few francs in his wallet, enough for the bus back to his mother's house.

When we got there he rang the doorbell while I stood a polite distance behind. She came running to open the door to the porch, throwing her arms around his neck and smothering him with kisses. 'My baby. You've come home! How wonderful.'

She picked up his bag and ushered him in. He followed her. Neither of them said anything to me. His mother was already summoning him into the kitchen where she promised she had his favourite dinner ready. He seemed to have forgotten all about me.

'Thomas?' My voice was a scared squeak. They both turned to look at me. The tiniest glimpse of annoyance crossed his features.

'Mama, this is Natacha. My girlfriend.'

I smiled my most engaging smile. She looked me up and down. I clearly wasn't what she had in mind for her son. She air-kissed me on both cheeks, the look of distaste on her face all too apparent.

'Come, I imagine you will be hungry too.' As I followed them, she turned to Thomas. 'So, does she know how to cook?' she asked as if I wasn't there.

That night we slept in Thomas's old bedroom. It was exactly as it was when he was a boy. Football and karate trophies lined the shelves; faded posters of racing drivers adorned the walls. I wondered if all boys in the 'system' world had bedrooms like this. If we'd had a normal childhood, would Marc have won football trophies too? The thought of Marc was too much and I started to cry.

Thomas was getting undressed. 'For god's sake, what's the matter with you?'

'I don't think your mother liked me.'

'Of course she did. You are so paranoid.'

But I wasn't. In the days that followed his mother progressed from her initial rude indifference to outright hostility towards me.

She doted on Thomas, treating him like her little prince. For his part, Thomas was happy to be waited on hand and foot, choosing to spend his days watching television. I felt trapped – I had escaped Réunion only to be marooned beside him on his mother's couch.

I felt as though it was a battle between Thomas's mother

and myself for who could be the most important woman in her son's life. She was determined to ensure it was her, not me.

We would close ourselves away in his bedroom and have whispered arguments. Even Thomas had to concede the situation was not healthy.

But things really came to a head when I came downstairs wearing a short skirt. She called me a tart, we started shouting at each other and it ended with her slapping me hard across the face.

I was mortified and told Thomas that if we didn't get our own place I would leave him. We agreed to move to Cannes, on the French Riviera – we hoped its glittering tourist industry would give us a good chance of finding work and establishing a place of our own.

His mother wept dreadfully the day we left. She shot me a look that said: 'You did this. See what you have done to me.'

I could barely contain my relief at leaving.

Cannes seemed like the fresh start we both needed. It was sunny, beautiful, glamorous and full of possibilities. Thomas went on benefits, appearing to have zero interest in working. We found a tiny little studio apartment, one room with a little kitchen. At last we had a place to call our own. I hoped happiness would soon follow.

For me this was the beginning of a long process of trying to work out how the world worked. Having been locked away in communes all my life the little things that people need to know to get through life were a mystery to me. Everything was a problem. For example, I needed to replace my French ID card before I could look for work. But I had no idea how to go about it. I didn't want Thomas to think I was stupid so I mostly tried to work it out for myself. It took me ages to figure out whom I needed to contact. Ringing them in my broken French to ask what documents I needed was horrible. The woman on the other end of the phone was impatient and told me to bring my birth certificate. But I didn't even know what a birth certificate was. I asked my dad but the one he had was from Thailand and was invalid. So I had to go through the whole process of trying to order an original. It was such a complex nightmare.

Thomas and I began talking about getting married and starting a family. I wanted to marry him, of course. But partly it felt like I needed to because marriage and children was part of my 'happily ever after' life plan. It's what I assumed normal people did.

I was shopping one day when I saw a 'help wanted' sign in a window. I went inside – mostly out of bored curiosity.

The store was lined with hundreds of pairs of designer sunglasses. An older woman stood behind the counter, smoking.

'Hello, darling. Can I help you?'

An enormous pair of bright red spectacles, the same colour as her abundant lipstick, framed her face.

'Hi,' I stammered, not sure what to say next. 'I've come about the job in the window?'

'Wonderful, darling, wonderful. Please, come. Sit down. My name is Manon. And you are?'

She held out a bejewelled hand in my direction. One of her rings was an enormous cluster of diamonds and emeralds.

'Natacha,' I said, awkwardly clasping her quiver of bright red fingernails.

'How charming. Tell me, darling, how much you know about sunglasses,' she asked expectantly.

'Um, not much,' I said, staring around the shop at the vast array of styles.

'But you can learn, yes?'

She was beaming at me in a very disarming way. We just clicked from that moment. By the time I left Manon's shop I was a full-time employee.

Thomas wasn't very receptive to the news of my job.

'Who will clean the flat and cook food?' he demanded. I thought he would be pleased to have the extra income.

'Well, we'll just have to share the cleaning. And it won't kill you to occasionally make your own dinner.'

'And what about the baby?'

'What baby? Thomas, I'm not pregnant. And we're not even married. At least this way we can save money for our wedding.'

I took his attitude as yet another sign of his controlling manner.

He tried a new tactic.

'Well, maybe there won't be a wedding. Maybe I'll throw you out on the street. Maybe I'll hook up with one of those bored rich sluts from the bars ...'

'Maybe you'll grow up, Thomas.'

That shut him up. He retreated to the couch and turned the television up loud.

At the shop, Manon quickly became my role model and confidante.

I shared with her my doubts about my relationship with Thomas, which, rather than improving, seemed to be in steady decline. He really wasn't the man I had hoped he was when we first met – in fact he was more of a boy than both Caleb and Jean-Yves put together.

Manon would listen to me patiently, nodding her head through clouds of cigarette smoke.

'But you are not his property, Natacha. There is no wedding certificate, his baby is not in your belly, nor his name tattooed on your arse … is it?' she asked, worried for a moment about what I might answer.

'No!' I burst out laughing. 'No, Manon, I promise you his name is not tattooed on my arse, or anywhere else for that matter.'

She really was a breath of fresh air, a world away from the submissive aunties I had grown up with.

She even helped me open a bank account by using her home address – something I had no idea how to do.

'A woman must have her own money, Natacha,' she counselled.

Each week I would deposit some of my wages into the account. We dubbed it my 'Escape from Thomas' fund.

His behaviour was becoming more controlling, aggressive and erratic. He seemed to resent my growing independence, still insisting that I should be at home full time to look after his every need.

On top of that he'd recently got interested in the occult, and he was starting to become a bit obsessed by it. He had a new group of friends who shared the interest. I found them all very creepy. I had only just escaped a fanatical cult, so even the merest hint of anything similar made me want to run a mile.

When my secret account hit 900 euros I knew it was time to go.

Manon and I went to a wine bar after work.

'So, little bird, time to fly free.' Manon poured me a large glass of white wine. I gulped it nervously.

'Is it? Am I really doing the right thing?'

She shrugged. 'You are young. You have a life to live. Yes, you haven't had it easy, but you are strong. It's poor old me I am sad for. I'll miss you, my dear.'

She was making a joke of it but I knew her words were heartfelt. I was going to miss her more than I could express. This woman had been my first friend in the outside world, a boss, a mentor and a surrogate parent all rolled into one. She'd given and taught me so much.

Despite our closeness I realised I still knew relatively little about her. She was divorced with a grown-up child still living in Montreal, Canada, which is where she was from. I had never found out why or how she came to be in Cannes. I suspected there was a sad story lurking underneath. I wanted to ask her but it felt intrusive.

'*Merde*, listen to me complaining. This is no time for sadness. A toast! To your future, Natacha. It's time for your bright light to shine.'

We clinked our glasses and drank.

As we hugged our final goodbyes it was almost unbearable. I already felt lost without my wise and funny friend.

I came home to find Thomas watching football at full volume as usual.

'Thomas, we need to talk.'

He didn't say anything.

'Thomas, can you turn that down, please. I need to speak to you.'

'I heard you the first time,' he snapped. 'Can't you see I'm watching a game?'

I grabbed the remote and switched the television off.

'What the fuck, Natacha?'

I took a deep breath.

'Thomas, I'm leaving you.'

I expected him to explode. Instead, he just looked at me with contempt and laughed.

'*You're* leaving *me*?'

He was on his feet. I took a step backwards.

'You're … leaving … *me*?' he repeated. It seemed to be sinking in. 'And going where? To do what?' He was beginning to boil. 'No one else would have you, you fucked up little bitch.'

'Don't you talk to me like that, you asshole.' Now I was getting angry. 'I've had enough of your bullshit, you control-freak mommy's boy. I'm not your servant – and from now on I'm not your girlfriend.'

'Fuck you, slut. Go on, get out then.'

He shoved me hard. I fell backwards into the doors that lead to the balcony. The back of my head connected with the toughened glass. My head spun and my vision was blurred. Thomas was dragging me up, his hands around my throat. He forced me back over the balcony ledge, squeezing my throat. I was terrified he was going to push me over the edge.

'Thomas, stop. I can't …' I was struggling so much for breath I couldn't speak.

The look of horror on my face snapped him back to sanity. He released his grip.

'Go on. Fuck off. Before I do something I really regret.'

I ran into the bedroom, throwing the contents of my wardrobe into a suitcase, followed by the contents of two drawers.

The cool air of the hallway helped clear my head. The football started again as I pulled the apartment door behind me.

There was a shout of rage and a crash as something solid smashed against the wall inside. That would be our Réunion photo – a memory of happier times.

I hurried off, dragging everything I owned with me.

I had done it.

Chapter 19

The Urban Jungle

London might as well have been the Amazon jungle. Only this time I knew for sure it was me who was the strange one.

The idea of moving around such a big city scared me witless. In Bangkok I'd lived behind high commune walls ringed with barbed wire, unable to see the street outside. Even when I went back there as an adult with Thomas I had hidden behind him for safety. And in Paris my greatest exposure to the city had been limited to a couple of glances from the back seat of a car.

I had found a room in a shared house with some other ex-cult members. I was grateful to have found a safe place to stay but I had very mixed feelings about taking their help. I felt as if I had lost my independence, everything I had worked for. Thomas and I had our own home; I'd even bought furniture.

Having been the cook, nanny and general cleaner at my parents' house for so many years I knew how to make myself useful, but it was made clear I'd need to pay my way.

The first time I went to the supermarket I got very carried away. After years of not having enough food the array of things on display was more temptation than I could bear. I fell for the fancy prepared food, anything which looked like the taste of luxury. I bought lots of bags of salad because pre-packed food was such a novelty to me, as was anything fresh and healthy. But I realised my mistake when I ended up having to throw most of it away because it went off so quickly.

Thomas was still hounding me. For the first few days he rang all the time – mostly at night, mostly drunk. Sometimes he begged me to come back. Other times he screamed down the phone that I was a messed-up bitch and no one else would have me. After a month his calls slowed down. After six weeks they stopped altogether.

Manon, ever the true friend, recommended me for a job in a London branch of the same chain of sunglasses stores we had worked for in France. I was taken on as a sales assistant in West London, earning the princely sum of £13,000 a year.

I was very grateful to her for fixing me up but I had a feeling this would be a different ballgame to the chilled-out little store in Cannes where it was just the two of us. I missed her wisdom and witticisms desperately.

I went to Primark to buy what I thought was a suitable outfit. As I stared at the racks of clothes I realised I had no idea what people wore to work. In Cannes it was fairly laid back, but this was a major city and I felt I ought to be smarter. In the end I settled for sensible-looking black trousers, a white fitted shirt and a grey cardigan. The night before I started I pored over the Underground map, plotting my route.

I also packed a large handbag, putting in a torch, a compass, a first aid kit, matches, a Swiss Army knife and water purification tablets – pretty much everything I thought I might need should the world end on my journey. The paranoia that it might was still very much ingrained in me.

One of my new housemates had written down instructions on how to use the ticket machines, but when my turn in the queue came I stood there clutching at my piece of paper helplessly. None of it made any sense. The man behind me yelled at me to get in the queue with a human station attendant instead. By the time I'd waited in both queues I was already late for work.

On the Tube I stared curiously at the other passengers, studying their clothes, their behaviour and the newspapers they read. They were fascinating. My curiosity was not well received. 'Want my photo or what?' snapped a grey-haired old lady.

Changing trains was so stressful I thought I would have a panic attack. I tried to follow the flow and keep up with the millions of signs at each change. At times I followed a crowd, thinking they must be going the same way as me, only to realise they were catching another connection. I only had two stations to go but I was so scared of the crowd that I let everyone else push in front of me. I missed two trains. I finally got the point and elbowed my way onto the third.

When I arrived at the shop, panting apologies, my new boss could see how flustered I was and made me a cup of tea. He introduced himself as Daniel, and a pretty blonde Irish girl called Simone. She was wearing a bubble-gum pink mini-dress and heels and long dangly earrings. She looked at my dowdy cardigan and shirt with obvious pity. I felt like a complete idiot for having bought such a dumb outfit.

The customers terrified me.

'Excuse me, Miss, can you help me?'

'Um … me?'

'Yes, you do work here, don't you?'

'Err, yeah.'

'Well, my friend bought a pair of these in tortoiseshell here last week.'

'OK …'

'Do you have any more in stock?'

'Um, I'm not sure.'

'Well, do you think you could check?'

'Yeah …'

I scurried into the stock room, pleased to be out of sight. It was dim and quiet in there. The rows of boxes were ordered and neat. It was calm, it made sense to me – unlike outside, which was busy and confusing.

I could feel the anxiety building inside me as I searched, running my finger down the labels on the boxes. The knot in my stomach tightened until I had to admit the glasses weren't there. I doubled back just to make sure I hadn't missed them. Finally I gave up. The thought of breaking the bad news to the customer made me feel sick.

'Where's the lady gone?'

'What lady?' said Daniel.

'Um … I'm really sorry. I went to look for some glasses, but she's gone.'

'So? It doesn't matter.'

Relief washed over me.

'Cool. Hey, we're having work drinks on Saturday. Like to come?'

The knot in my stomach was back. Somehow his wavy blond hair and blue eyes made it hard to refuse.

'Yeah, I guess so.'

'Wicked.'

The drinks were in a wine bar in Putney. Simone had kindly given me her *A-Z* street map; I was really pleased with myself when I got there without a drama. As I walked in Daniel was at the bar. A pair of outrageously made-up women stood next to him, sipping white wine. I couldn't take my eyes off them.

'Thinking of expanding your horizons?' asked Daniel playfully.

I didn't know what he was talking about. I was about to nod inanely in agreement when he let me off the hook.

'They're geezers,' he said under his breath.

'What?' Now it made sense.

'Blokes. Don't worry, they won't bite. Not unless you ask them to.'

I felt foolish and shuffled a little uncomfortably.

'Boss always gets the first round in – what are you having? Simone, what about you?' Daniel called across the room to the table.

'Rum and coke, please.'

I copied: 'Same for me too, thanks.'

At the table Daniel introduced me to his friend Felix.

'So you're the new girl, then?' He winked at Daniel. 'Prettier than Simone.'

Simone pulled a face and swatted at him with a beer mat. I smiled along with the joke, but found the humour – banter, as they called it – a bit bemusing.

'So, Natacha,' said Daniel. 'You grew up in Thailand, right?'

Felix jumped in. 'You grew up in Thailand? My mate and

I are going there in January. What's it like? Where are the good spots?'

I could feel three pairs of expectant eyes on me. I started taking short gulps of air to suppress the rising panic.

'It's nice.'

It was an abusive hell. I nearly lost my mind. And I don't have a bloody clue about Thailand, only the inside of the compounds I lived in.

'Nice? I bet it's amazing. What did your parents do?'

'My dad was an aid worker.'

He was a Shepherd in a Christian sex cult.

'Oh, wow. I always wanted to do aid work,' Simone chimed in.

'Giving tramps hand-jobs in bus shelters doesn't count, Simone.'

'No, Felix, but it always cheers your dad up.'

I hoped for a moment an argument was going to break out, sparing me from answering more questions, but they both fell about laughing instead, something that perplexed me even more. Felix had been so rude to her but Simone seemed to find it genuinely funny. In the end they bought my vague answers and the conversation moved on.

'What are we doing with Iraq? Tony Blair is a sick joke,' said Felix.

'Yeah, but you didn't bother to vote, did you? Don't complain if you are too apathetic to care,' chided Simone.

'*Touché*. You got me on that one.'

I tried to keep up. I knew who Tony Blair was but only because I had seen him on the news and worked out he was the British Prime Minister. I didn't understand what they meant by voting. And I had read something in the newspaper about a war in Iraq. I had worried whether it was another sign of the impending End Time.

Their conversation had jumped again. They were talking about someone called Nelson Mandela.

'He's just so awesome. Man, what a dude.'

I had no idea who he was. The only personalities or celebrities I knew of were the ones David Berg had promoted. The two that had stuck in my mind were Mother Theresa, because she was a Christian and an example of sacrifice, and Colonel Gaddafi, whom Berg had met and described as a 'great leader' because he opposed the USA.

Since leaving home and moving in with Thomas I had tried to educate myself. If I got caught out and heard someone talking about a figure or a place I didn't know I looked it up so I knew for next time. I was intelligent, I knew I was. But I felt like an uneducated simpleton. And I hated the fact that people might think I was.

My head was spinning from the drink and trying to keep up.

Now Daniel and Felix were arguing about football.

'Beckham is an idiot. He shouldn't have lost his temper.'

'Yeah, but Fergie hates him, doesn't he? That's not his fault.'

Sport and the way people spent so much time debating it was so strange to me. Why did people care so much about it? I think I worked out Beckham might be a player, but I still couldn't work out who the Fergie person was.

Simone seemed to get the impression my frown meant I was just bored with the boys' sport chat, so I was grateful when she changed the subject back to a subject I could actually answer.

'So, Natacha, what was Cannes like, then? Is it super glam?'

Later that evening we all went back to Daniel's flat to carry on the party.

'Your future's so bright, you gotta wear shades,' he sang, shaking his hips.

I giggled at the irony as much as his funny little dance.

'Did you know this song's actually about nuclear war?'

A peel of laughter just burst out of me. Really loud, inappropriately loud. Almost maniacal. Nuclear war! Of course it was!

'Yah, but it's not meant to be funny, Natacha.'

I just stood there rocking with the black humour of it – even here Heaven's Girl was still stalking me.

As the night wore on I downed several rum and cokes. I didn't like the taste but with each one I started to feel fuzzier and more confident, dancing wildly round the living room with Simone. When Daniel handed me a joint I took it.

When I woke up several hours later I was fully clothed and covered with a duvet. 'Morning, beautiful.'

Daniel. He was lying next to me, wearing only a pair of boxer shorts.

My bladder hurt so much I thought it would explode. I wanted to cry.

'What a night. Blimey, you can't half pack it away.'

I felt the nausea rise in my throat.

'Felix seemed taken with you. I told him "hands off, she's my employee".'

My leg started to spasm.

'How pissed was Simone? I had to beg the taxi driver to take her. He was worried she'd throw up in his cab. Daft cow. She always drinks her own bodyweight in Bacardi.'

My chest tightened. I couldn't breathe.

'Are you all right, babe? Don't stress. We've all got hangovers.'

I couldn't move.

'Ah, I get it. Nah, don't be daft. Nothing happened. You've still got all your clothes on. You wiped out on the sofa so I put you to bed. I was a good boy. Come on, I'll even make you a coffee. Bathroom's just down the hall to the left, by the way.'

My legs sprang back to life. I rushed to the bathroom just in time to lift the toilet lid and heave into the bowl.

Bit by bit I started to cope with work and find my way around the city. But inside I was a jumble of angst.

For a while I went Goth – I could identify with the gloomy style. I dyed my hair black and painted my nails black to match my lipstick. I don't really know what motivates Goths to dress the way they do – I didn't really care. For me it was an outward expression of how I felt inside.

But I didn't like the strange looks I would get from people, so I moved on to bright orange leopard prints and slicked-back hair, a look that I thought screamed Confidence! I dropped it after someone on a bus called me a chav. I wasn't sure what a chav was but the tone in the man's voice had made me pretty sure I didn't want to be one. And I was definitely sure I didn't want to look like someone who attracted abuse from strangers. I reinvented myself in an American preppy style. I looked like a walking Gap advert. I thought it made me look like someone who was clean-cut and going somewhere. Next I tried the sexy French girl look. I put blonde streaks through my hair and dressed in little mini-skirts and ballet pumps. I played up my Frenchness. I guess this was my sassy phase, waving my cigarette around and saying *Oh la la*! I patently sounded ridiculous because I had an American accent. To cover for that I continued with the lie I had told Felix and Daniel about my dad being an aid worker.

None of it had anything to do with fashion. Each look was about my trying find a personality. It's hard to build an identity around an outfit – no matter how hard you might want to.

In a moment of self-loathing I cut all my hair off, which was awful because I felt ugly for weeks afterwards. I had no friends and no one to confide in.

On the few occasions I called home my mother just urged me to 'get the victory' or to pray harder. It was all I could do not to slam the phone down on her.

All I could afford to eat was instant noodles with the occasional cheap bottle of wine that I would drink alone in my bedroom while listening to weepy love songs. I would spend hours looking at myself in the mirror, trying to fathom who I was. Hardly the glamorous 'system' life.

My first Christmas in London was strange but nice. It felt lovely just to be relaxed and watch films on TV. I was obsessed by *The Simpsons* cartoon. I loved how Bart got away with being so naughty all the time. But I still had to work out how a 'system' Christmas worked. Simone at work had bought me an Advent calendar but I didn't know what it was. I assumed it was a kind of decoration and left it on my dressing table unopened. It was only when I came to tidy it away that a chocolate fell out and I realised you were meant to open a door for each day of the month. It was the same with the crackers. I snapped mine in half myself because

I didn't know you were supposed to pull it with another person.

From the moment I woke up I was tense and nervous, but I tried to get through each day without embarrassing myself, quickly working out that if if I spoke as little as possible to as few people as possible and turned down social invites my chances of humiliation were significantly reduced.

Despite this I didn't do too badly at work and I was moved to the flagship store in Bond Street. Every day I walked past shops with an array of consumer goods on display, offering a tantalising glimpse of luxuries I was denied.

By then I'd learned to dress better but I still felt tiny compared to the chic, well-dressed women who came into the store. To me they were materialistic bitches, especially the ones who let their boyfriends buy their sunglasses. I was conditioned to believe a woman's place was to give everything but expect nothing.

My whole life had been a countdown to my day of glory at Armageddon. Facing the fact that there was no martyr's paradise and no solid gold mansion was a crushing realisation.

I had this constant nagging voice: *What if I have just turned my back on my destiny? What if they were right?*

Every time I turned on the TV and saw news of an air crash or an earthquake I went cold with fear. *Has Armageddon started without me?*

On my way to a training day at head office I travelled by rail through Buckinghamshire. I was absolutely captivated as I looked out of the carriage window at a series of quiet little towns and the rows of houses with neatly clipped hedges, smart curtains and cars parked in the drives. I played a game with myself, trying to imagine who lived in them.

I wasn't greedy. I didn't need luxury. I wanted a home, a family, stability and safety. Knowing how to get there was the hard part.

Chapter 20

The Prince Is Dead

The knocking woke me up. Rain was pounding at the windows and a gale howled outside.

'Natacha, get up.' The voice was urgent.

'Whaaaa. It's my day off; it's OK.'

'Get up! We are all down here. Come down.'

I was shattered, veering between irritation and dread. The night Matt phoned to tell me of Marc's death his voice had had the same flat urgency.

I groaned as I threw on a dressing gown and went downstairs. 'Is everyone OK?'

My housemates were sitting on the sofa, looking confused.

A girl called Sarah spoke. 'My parents called me early this morning. Davidito is dead. He murdered someone and then shot himself.'

It had been so long since I had heard the name that for a moment I struggled to work out whom she was talking about.

'Davidito. Davidito? As in Prince Davidito?'

She frowned and nodded. 'Yes. Isn't it awful? I can't understand it. Why would he do that?'

I sat down, trying to take it all in. Davidito had been a key figure of my childhood. He was the little boy in the picture book *The Story of Davidito*. He was The Family's leader-in-waiting, the chosen one and our general at the battle of Armageddon. He was the boy I had been so jealous of that I hated him, but since leaving The Family I hadn't really given him a second thought.

'Come to think of it …' I had a moment of clarity. 'When did he even last get a mention in a Maria letter?'

Sarah shook her head, thinking about it for a minute. 'He definitely got talked about at Victor Camp when I was there. He was playing up, apparently. I remember it because Maria called the house they lived in the house of the open pussy.'

I let out a bitter little laugh. 'Why doesn't that surprise me? But he murdered someone? Are you sure?'

'Brutally. The worst bit is that they think he was trying to kill his own mother. But instead he killed one of her friends, Angela Smith. I'm not sure who she is. But poor woman, he slashed her throat. They were trying to arrest him but he shot himself. What a murderous coward.'

I had a sudden flash of angry loyalty towards my prince. 'Just hang on. We don't know the circumstances yet. Why would he hurt someone for no reason?'

I called my parents, who were as shocked and confused as I was. They told me Mama Maria had put out a very brief, business-like statement to all Shepherds, confirming the events and expressing condolence for the 'much loved' murdered woman. She'd said virtually nothing about her dead son except that he'd been 'corrupted by outside forces' – something I suspected was tellingly cold.

I went to a local Internet café to try to find out more. The story was all over the US media. Bit by bit I learned that most recently he'd been living with his mother in Portugal, which is where her secret leadership HQ had been based. Most of his childhood had been spent constantly moving around with Grandpa and Maria. They'd spent time in Portugal and also in the Philippines, but because Grandpa was a wanted man in several countries they didn't ever stay anywhere too long. Davidito's childhood had been hell, his every thought and move monitored and controlled to mould him into the perfect prince.

I honestly could not believe what I was reading. I learned he had fallen in love with a young woman called Alexia. They met in a commune in Europe and fell in love and married within the group. But Davidito was of course expected to set a good example, meaning he and Alexia were ordered to 'share' each other sexually with others. It was something the two young people, who only wanted to be with each other, hated. In the year 2000 they ran away. Davidito went so far as to put out a statement saying, 'We cannot continue to condone or be party to what we feel is an abusive, manipulative organisation that teaches false doctrine … You have devoured God's sheep, ruining people's lives by propagating false doctrines and advocating harmful practices in the name of God, and as far as I can see, show no regret or remorse.'

My parents claimed they had no idea about this. At a time when Mama Maria was labelling teens who left as 'apostates' or 'backsliders', the embarrassment of her own son leaving was something she had done her utmost to hush up.

He got a job as an electrician and called himself Ricky Rodriguez in an attempt to build a new life. But he was deeply depressed and consumed with rage. He felt his 'mission' was to find his mother and bring her to justice. But when other second-generation ex-members of The Family began contacting him he snapped and hatched a plan to murder her. He got as far as Angela Smith, one of his former nannies.

With a bolt of horrible realisation I worked out who Angela was. She was in *The Story of Davidito*, naked with the little prince during their 'love-up sessions'. I felt sickened as I read how since ten months' old poor Davidito had been 'initiated' into sex, used as a twisted experiment by all the adults around him – men and women.

Before committing the murder Davidito had recorded a suicide video. Someone had put it on YouTube. He spoke of his mission: 'There's this need that I have. It's not a want. It's a need for revenge. It's a need for justice, because I can't go on like this.' Calm and lucid, he stared at the camera, his hatred for his mother ringing out loud and clear: 'Well, Mom's gonna pay. She's gonna pay dearly … you're a sick fucking pervert, and you don't have anything better to do with your life than to fuck up your little kids …'

Tears ran down my face as he went on. It was as if he was talking to me directly: 'Ah, I've tried so many things trying to somehow fit in. Somehow to find, you know, a normal life. Everybody who I talked to about this says, "Well, you know, everybody has their problems." But those people who say that don't have a clue as to what actually went on. I mean, 'coz they weren't part of the cult.'

For me it was patently clear the abuse had caused him to do what he did. But, as always, The Family refused to admit the truth, blaming the usual – the system and the devil – for corrupting him. I realised for the first time just what an evil man Grandpa was. And Mama Maria? She was sick.

I was consumed with rage at my parents. How could they not have known? I was just a child when I saw the Davidito book. They were adults. How could they not have recognised what filth it contained? They both went into denial, insisting they had no idea children were abused. They kept saying they couldn't get their heads around it and needed to see evidence. I was incandescent. What more evidence did they need?

'But what about the book?' I spat at my father over the telephone. 'Did you think those pictures were normal?'

He sounded crestfallen. 'We were hippies, Natacha. I didn't understand it.'

My father tried to make it better by reassuring us that he'd never taken those publications as something to be copied. If he felt that, surely so would the majority of others. 'If bad things happened, then I am sure it only happened in Father David's house,' was his rationale.

'Oh no, Daddy. It happened. And it happened to me too.'

Finally I told him all about Clay. The line went silent.

'Why didn't you tell us?'

I snorted with derision. 'Tell? Did you ever see what happened to the kids who told?'

I gave up the conversation. It was going nowhere. I knew they were genuinely devastated by my revelations, but I was in no mood to forgive.

Poor little tragic Prince Davidito had died his martyr's death just as prophesied. And to me he had in a way died fighting the Antichrist. But it wasn't the system that was evil; it was The Family.

In the coming weeks I spent every spare hour in that Internet café furiously Googling any information I could find. Websites set up by ex-members had sprung up, detailing story after story of abuse, beatings and brainwashing. It felt comforting to know I wasn't alone, but it sickened me to my core to know that my family had spent our lives as part of something so terrible.

But much worse was to come. Next Davida went public with her story. She was the daughter of Sara, one of Davidito's nannies and the main author of *The Story of Davidito*. Davida's father was Alfred, Grandpa's personal assistant. She and Davidito had been brought up to call each other brother and sister, but she claimed they had been forced into sexual contact with each other from a very young age. Grandpa was obsessed about continuing his own bloodline, so Davidito had also allegedly been forced to have sex with Mene, Grandpa's granddaughter. Most horrifyingly of all, Davida went so far as to claim Davidito also had sex with his own mother – Mama Maria. I almost vomited on the floor when I heard that. But, as usual, my parents defended her, pointing out that she fiercely denied this was true. This is something she continues to deny to this day.

Yet for me the truth was darker. In the early 1990s Davidito had been forced to undergo psychological evaluations to 'prove' that childhood sex with adults had no negative effect on him.

I felt sick to my guts as I remembered how in France we had got on our knees to pray for The Family to win a big court case in London. That had happened in 1995 and concerned grandparents who had attempted to win custody of their grandson from their cult-member daughter.

I typed it into Google. And there it was, all over the Net. In his summing up the judge had clearly stated that child abuse was rife within The Family.

Yet inexplicably, after a major PR offensive by The Family, the child was returned back to them. After the court case ended Mama Maria had issued a lukewarm apology, blaming any abuse on a handful of members who had 'misinterpreted' Grandpa's teachings.

To me this was absolute rubbish.

As if all this wasn't enough for me to take in, I found out what had happened to Mene – the inspiration for my role model Heaven's Girl. The poor girl had been tortured and abused to the point of insanity. She had a breakdown and was eventually shipped off to live with her grandmother.

It hit me that this was also something the adults must have known about. What about the Mene letters I'd studied in Word Time? Didn't we learn that she'd been beaten for her own good? To help her? These people were depraved.

Everything I thought I knew, everything I ever believed, had been taken away from me. It was as if a huge rug had been pulled out from underneath me and all that was left was a gaping black hole.

My own life was falling apart. A couple of months earlier I had left the relative safety of the sunglasses store and got a job in a mobile phone store. My new boss was a nasty bully. She was a spinster and seemed to be very bitter and twisted about the fact that she'd never married. She hated me on sight and found fault with everything I did. She yelled at me constantly, but the worst was when she threw some lever-arch files at my head. A few days after that she made a joke in front of the other staff that she wanted to punch me so hard that it would send me over a building.

After weeks of coming home in tears I was signed off sick. I plucked up the courage to bring an internal grievance against her, probably the first time I'd ever stood up for myself, but when it was time to decide whether to take my case to a full employment tribunal I backed out and quit my job. I didn't have the confidence or strength to go through with it and I just wanted out by that stage.

The pressure to find new employment was immense, not least because I now had Vincent to look out for. He was the latest escapee to what we laughingly nicknamed 'the back-sliders safe house'. Vincent was 17 now and had just come out as gay. My parents struggled with it at first because male homosexuality was considered an excommunicable offence within The Family, but they tried to accept it. I didn't care as long as he was happy. He was rebelling in a general teenage way, and smoking weed in his secret reading hideout at the bottom of the garden. My parents didn't really know how to deal with him, so they suggested he join me in London. It was great to see him, but I felt that the weight of the added responsibility was very unfair. After all, who would have to be there for him when things went wrong? Having left the cult he was on his own, as we all were. Our parents relinquished their parental responsibilities and I knew that it would be up to me to take care of Vincent.

I had been awake all night, tossing and turning. At 5 a.m. I got up and went for a walk in the park near our flat. It was probably stupidly dangerous for a woman to walk alone in a pitch-black London park, but I didn't care. I took my CD Walkman and sat on a bench, playing the Kelly Clarkson song 'Behind These Hazel Eyes' over and over again, revelling in my misery.

Everything I had tried so hard to become was beyond me. I couldn't fix myself into the person I wanted to be. I couldn't be normal.

By 6 a.m. joggers and dog walkers started to fill the park. I didn't care who saw me. I put on my sunglasses and just carried on crying. I felt like I wanted to scream out loud, to just walk up a mountain and fling myself off it.

It was 7 a.m. when I walked back home. As I turned my key in the door I heard the sound of crying coming from the kitchen.

Vincent was sitting at the table; he looked up at me with frightened eyes. Blood ran from his nose, and his cheeks were covered with scratches.

'Natacha, I'm sorry. I'm sorry. They hurt me.'

As I held him, he poured out the sordid tale. Two men he had met in a bar had tricked him into walking into a park where they attacked him, kicking him to the ground and assaulting him. He was badly hurt, but he refused to let me call the police.

I cleaned his face up as best I could, made him a hot drink and put him to bed, wincing at the sight of his bloodied clothes. I picked them up and took them into the bathroom to wash them. As I scrubbed at them I started to shake. I couldn't stop shaking. My whole body was convulsed. I gripped the sink for support and stared at my reflection with hatred. All I could see was how useless, ugly, stupid, poisoned, twisted and mad I was.

A couple of weeks later I was on the Underground, coming back from an unsuccessful job interview, when I started to fantasise about throwing myself onto the track.

I thought about how easy it could be and the relief I would feel. When the next stop came my legs carried me off the train as if sleepwalking.

I stood on the platform swaying, gearing myself to jump, when I felt a hand on my arm. 'Can I help you?' said a woman's voice. 'Are you going to faint?'

Her voice brought me back to reality. I ran away from her and up the escalators. Outside the station I leaned against a wall as violent shakes came over me again. I wanted to cry but nothing came out; I was numb with shock at my own actions.

For the first time since leaving the cult I needed God, calling out to him: 'Jesus, where are you? Please. Help me. Please tell me what to do.'

Around a week later I had the house all to myself for the evening. Vincent was at a friend's, and the housemates had gone to the cinema. I remember watching TV; there was a soap opera about a happy family who all loved each other. It made me depressed to watch it. I swigged from a bottle of wine, getting angrier and angrier, until I threw the remote at the screen.

I tried to sleep, pulling the duvet over my head. I couldn't relax so I sat up in bed drinking more wine from the bottle. When that ran out I stumbled into the kitchen, pulling open the food cupboards to find more booze. In the back of one I found some vodka. I took a large swig straight from the bottle.

I went back into my bedroom and put my music on at full blast.

There was a rapping at the door. I ignored it, but it got louder, more persistent. I opened it to see the elderly man who lived next door.

'Yes. Can I help you?'

He looked a bit embarrassed. He never looked very comfortable around us.

'Your music is very loud. Would you mind turning it down?'

'No, it's not.'

'Sorry?'

'I said, no, it's not. It's not loud.'

He coughed. 'I'm afraid it is. Would you mind awfully . . .?'

'Oh, go fuck yourself.'

I slammed the door shut in his face. I'd never in my life been so rude to someone before, and for a minute I thought it was hysterically funny. I ran back to my bedroom and turned it up even louder, laughing my head off.

Then I realised what I'd done and I was mortified. I turned the music off and looked at myself in the mirror.

'You stupid, rude bitch. What did you talk to him like that for? Who the hell are you? What have you become?'

The face looking at me was ugly, angry, contorted. 'Ugly bitch. Go away.' I threw my hairbrush at my reflection, hurling insults at myself: 'Backsliding bitch, stupid, useless, pointless bitch. What is the fucking point of you?'

Very calmly I walked into the kitchen and grabbed a ball of string. I took it into the living room with the intent of hanging myself from the light fixture.

As if choosing a piece of meat in a butcher's shop, I assessed the light and the rope. The rope was too thin.

I went back into my room and got the vodka. Then I went back into the kitchen and poured myself a long drink, this time mixing it with lemonade. Inside I was as cold as the ice cubes I put in it.

I took the string and sat at the kitchen table with a pair of scissors. Slowly and deliberately I cut three very long pieces and began to braid them together to make a rope that would be thick enough to take my body weight.

I must have sat there for an hour braiding it. I was crying but I was so scarily calm.

It crossed my mind that this was going to be a painful way to die, but that was small fry compared with the thought of going on living.

When the rope was ready I walked back to the living room and began to tie it to the light fitting. Everything was in place and I was just about to tie it round my neck when Marc's face flashed into my mind.

I screamed out to myself. 'What the hell are you doing, Natacha?'

I ran back into the kitchen. My hands were so shaky I could barely pick up the receiver. I dialled my parents' number.

My mother answered. 'Mommy, it's me. I just tried to kill myself.'

She started crying and telling me she loved me. But as usual she didn't really know what to say.

She passed the phone to my dad.

'Natacha, what on earth are you doing? Don't be so stupid. Are you drunk? Calm down and take some deep breaths.'

He was kind but quite tough. It was the kick up the ass I needed. I must have spoken to him for over an hour, and by the time I hung up I was feeling better. I collapsed into a very disturbed sleep.

I woke up with the mother of all hangovers. But my mind was already clear about the next course of action. I maxed out my credit card and bought a return ticket to Réunion.

I didn't really think about the consequences of it until I was in the cab to the airport. That's when the enormity of it hit me. I'd failed at work, at London, at life. I'd arrived in this city at my absolute lowest – depressed after the break-up with Thomas, grieving for Marc and with no idea what to do with my life. I was running on autopilot, still a clone of the cult, with no real idea of what made me tick.

I think I began to understand that all I had really done was run away from my problems. My self-hatred, spite towards my parents and bitterness towards God were destroying me.

I tried to convince myself going back was a kind of pilgrimage. I made a vow that I'd face my demons, deal with my parents and be back in London within the month.

Chapter 21

Reincarnation

The wind tugged at my loose shirt, blowing tangled hair into my eyes. I let out an anguished wail, but my voice disappeared into the stormy night. Tropical rain pounded the tiny bedroom window ledge I was perched on. Tears streamed down my cheeks and into my mouth. I could taste their saltiness.

I was drunk – very drunk.

I stood with my arms outstretched as the wind buffeted my body. I was cursing and shouting, swearing and crying. The concrete patio was a long way below but I honestly didn't care if I lived or died.

'I hate you, God. I hate you. I hate you, Jesus. I hate you too, Grandpa. You bastard. You evil, sick, lying pervert. All of it was a lie. You lied to me!'

I stood there vocalising all the hate, the deep-seated hurt and my anger and grief at Marc's death.

I wanted to fall.

I let go and toppled backwards, falling onto my mattress. I landed safely on my bed – but my sense of helplessness fell in the other direction, smashing into a thousand pieces on the concrete. It felt good. Cathartic. A thousand hurts poured away, as if I had lanced a boil of emotion.

When I woke the next morning the storm had blown itself out. Somehow mine had too. I had a new clarity.

I could see my parents for the flawed personalities they were – blinded by their faith and brainwashed after years of submission to group rules but not bound by wickedness. Their mistake had been to believe in Grandpa (David Berg) and Mama Maria (whose real name I now knew was Karen Zerby). For me they were truly twisted psychopaths who ran The Family for their own ends. But my parents still hadn't lost their faith in the cult, even after all the Davidito revelations. They insisted The Family had learned its lesson and was now changed for the better. I too accepted that not everyone in the group was bad; there were many good, honest and kind people, and so I wanted to believe their assurances.

My mother had just given birth again, to baby Brian. She thought he was a gift sent from Marc in heaven and as such she idolised him.

Her elegant beauty still shined, but she was tired and worn down from a life of constant childbearing.

'I wouldn't change a thing, Natacha,' she insisted.

I wished I could say the same.

'When are you going to find a husband, settle down and have babies? Maybe this is why you are so unhappy. Is the "system" life really what you want? Turning your back on God has not given you what you wanted, has it?'

She really thought she knew what was best for me. She always did.

I wanted to leave Réunion and strike out on my own again. But as I walked barefoot on the island's sandy beaches the thought of going back to another London winter filled me with dread.

My mother was not long back from a short visit to a Family commune in South Africa. She was full of zeal and stories of a group of young people she had met who were doing God's work there.

'You'd like it, Natacha,' she enthused. 'The Family is doing a lot of aid work, helping the poor build their lives. The need is so great. It's not like it was when you were a child. Mama Maria has really changed things. Everything in the homes is so relaxed and fun now. I think you'd fit right in. And there are some very handsome young men, too,' she said knowingly.

Little by little she wore away at me until I began to think she might be right.

'It would do you good, get you out of this rut you're in. You tried the "system" life. It hurt you. Giving your life to Jesus is the way to heal your pain.'

As I wrote my diary that evening, I tried to get my head straight.

'I know the Lord will work everything out for me but I am scared I will find myself in a position I can't get out of. I must be very weak to even think about going back to the group. But the Lord will make the right decision for me.'

I took my return ticket to London out of the drawer and ripped it to pieces, only to instantly regret it and Sellotape it back together again. I was all over the place. But I made a decision to put my faith in Jesus and let him decide.

My mother sniffed victory. She put me in contact with Paul, a man my age living in the South Africa commune.

We began exchanging emails. He seemed nice, very devout and on fire for God. I was really beginning to think I might have found someone to build a future with. But as our correspondence developed and our emails became more intimate, he started to show a very unpleasant side. He became increasingly obsessed with sex. He would tell me all the different things he wanted to do to me. It was supposed to be sexy and a turn-on. He assumed that the moment I landed I would fall into his bed and swear my undying love for him. He also was very clear that any wife of his would be expected to 'share' – I took that to mean that he wanted to do the same. It left me angry and a bit sickened. Why did everything about our version of Christianity always seem to end up being about sex?

A few weeks later I was walking home – I'd been out with a local friend from the Thomas days to hear a jazz trio at one of the local bars. We had a few drinks, a few laughs, and I left feeling quite upbeat, even normal. A tall man I didn't recognise approached me just off the main strip.

'Excuse, Miss, can you tell me where I can get a drink this time of night?'

I pointed politely at the bar I had just left.

'Yeah, great. Cheers. Oh. One more thing.'

I nodded, enjoying the exchange.

Out came a knife.

'Where can I get a fuck around here?'

He grabbed me by the throat and shoved me into an alley.

'Please,' I choked. 'Don't do this.'

'Shut up and get your shorts off.'

I'd thought about this moment often. All those years reading *Heaven's Girl* and watching her submit to the Antichrist's troops. She even managed to say 'I love you' as the soldiers took turns. Now it was my test.

I tried to speak, but my mouth was so dry with fear my tongue stuck to the roof of it.

'What? Didn't you hear me, bitch? Do as I say or I'll stab you.'

He ran the knife under my breasts to make his point.

'Please don't hurt me. I'm a Christian. Please don't do this.'

He gave me a sneer of hate. Amazed at my own calmness, I carried on talking.

'You don't have to do this, because if you hurt me you will only hurt yourself.'

He relaxed his grip on me a little.

'You're a nutter, lady.'

'We can talk instead. Please don't hurt me. Let's just talk.'

He was getting confused.

'Stop messing with my head and get your clothes off, bitch. We're gonna have some fun.'

'No,' I said with surprising firmness. 'Are you OK? Are you upset with someone?'

'What?' he snapped.

'What's upsetting you? Why do you want to hurt me?' I wasn't begging or pleading. I amazed myself at how calm my voice sounded.

'Because you asked for it.' But at the same time as he said it he lowered his knife. 'You stay here, though, right? We'll talk.'

'Yes, I promise.'

'You aren't fucking going anywhere.'

'I won't. I'll stay.'

My brain was working on full alert. I was beginning to understand his psychology and what I needed to do to stay alive.

'So what do you want to talk about?'

'Nothing. Just shut up. Sit there.' He pointed to the wall.

I sat down as he sat next to me. He pointed the knife again but this time it was more of a sweeping gesture than a stabbing movement.

I sat in silence, thoughts whizzing through my head.

I could see the roof of our house from where I was standing. It was so close I could hear Gypsy barking in the front garden. Should I try to seize a chance to run? I realised that if I did I wouldn't get very far in my heels. Should I keep talking? Above all else I knew I had to keep him calm.

After a while he started talking. I asked him about his family and he told me about his mother, whom he said he loved. I asked him how he would feel if someone treated his mother the way he had treated me. His expression changed from threatening to regretful.

'I'm going to go now, OK?' I said, moving slowly away.

'OK.'

All his anger had gone.

'Hey, Miss. I'm sorry if I hurt you. I didn't mean to, OK?'

'I know you didn't.'

'Don't you dare report me. If you do I'll find you and hurt you, I swear.'

'I won't. I promise.'

At that he turned and left, and I ran. When I got home I was hysterical and told my father what had just happened. He got straight in his car and drove the streets for hours trying to find a man who fitted the description I had given him, but to no avail.

I felt dirty, ashamed and subconsciously convinced that it was my fault. If only I hadn't been to the bar, if only I hadn't been wearing such revealing clothes. The attack brought back all the old feelings of self-hatred I had felt as a child.

I was scared to go out at night now. Even during the day I jumped every time I heard a male voice or a man walking past me in the street.

My parents had finally entered the digital age and we had the Internet at home. To keep myself from dying of boredom I started to spend a lot of time logging onto various chat-rooms. That's how I met John, an IT salesman from Wales.

He was funny and flirty and I began to think he might be a soul mate. We spent hours talking online. He told me all about Wales and his job, which sounded impressive. I told him a little bit about myself (but not about the cult). I did admit to him how hard I had found London life and how lost I had felt in the big city. He listened and encouraged me to try again, telling me that I'd get used to it, and to live my dreams.

My conversations with him made me realise rejoining the cult and moving to South Africa would be a big mistake. Going backwards and getting trapped in The Family again was something I would regret.

Mom cried when I told her and begged me to reconsider. 'But look at what you are leaving. You could devote your life to God. Instead you are going back to an empty, shallow existence? Why?'

Why indeed?

It wasn't only meeting John that had changed something in me. I had replayed the attempted rape over and over in my head a thousand times, and as I did so something shifted in my perception. I stopped blaming myself and accepted it could have happened to any woman. But, more importantly,

I realised how my quick thinking and fast talking had prevented the man from actually raping me. I had talked him down and stopped him hurting me. My wits had saved me. When I looked at it like that I couldn't help but feel a growing sense of confidence in my ability to survive any obstacle.

When my plane touched down in London after a 14-month absence I felt stronger and more confident than I ever had. This time I pulled my luggage trolley through Heathrow with my head held high. The rhythm and pulse of the city no longer left me sweating with nerves; it felt right, real and solid. I blended in with ease, no longer the alien species.

John took leave and came to stay with me for a few days. He was as good looking as I had hoped, dark, rugged and well-built. But the rest of it was a nightmare. All he wanted to do was get drunk. If I thought it was going to be a fairytale romance he drowned that illusion very quickly. On day three we sat in the pub watching rugby as he downed his seventh pint of lager. As I looked over at him with disappointment I wondered what it was in me that still felt the need to have a man rescue me.

I stood up and told John I wanted to go immediately. When we got back home I told him it was over and asked him to leave. It was a disappointment, but ending our brief romance ultimately made me feel empowered. Finally I was making the decisions I needed to take control of my life.

Others were beginning to notice my new confidence too. I found a job in HR, which I loved. I socialised at work and developed a nice bunch of girlfriends, even confiding in one or two of them about my past. That was a big step, but they didn't reject me or call me a freak. They just accepted me for who I was.

Slowly but surely I was beginning to accept it too.

I'd pretty much given up on men by the time a tall, sandy-haired guy approached me in the pub one evening. I couldn't help but notice that his million-dollar smile masked a distinct nervousness. I liked that. I liked the idea of being a woman of whom men thought highly enough to be nervous around. I used to be the nervous, tongue-tied one, and the change of roles felt good.

'Are you on Facebook?' he asked.

I laughed out loud. 'Yes. Why?'

'I thought maybe I could send you a friend request?'

'What a line. Why don't you just ask for my phone number instead?'

Once Kevin's nerves settled down he turned out to be funny, balanced and totally at ease with himself. He didn't have anything to prove; he didn't have a desire to control me or manipulate me. He was just … normal.

We'd been dating for about six months – it was all very nice, and definitely the first time I had allowed myself to take a relationship one step at a time. There was no instant declaration of love, no getting carried away with myself and planning what we'd call our children after only a week of knowing him. We took it slowly and it felt like a very healthy way to get to know someone.

But after six months things began to get more serious and I knew I had to tell him the truth about my upbringing. I could keep up my charade indefinitely, but doing so might drive me to madness. And if we had any hope of a proper future then I had to let him know. I also liked him so much I wanted him to know all about the real me. There was a risk he would dump me – I couldn't blame him if he did – but I had no choice but to take that chance and confess all.

One summer's afternoon we sat drinking rosé wine on a blanket in his garden. It was so pleasant I almost didn't want to spoil the mood. But I had to.

There's no easy way to tell the man you're staking your future on about a childhood like mine: the secret life of skewed Christianity, the End Time Army, the superpowers, the violent abuse, the molestation, the guilt, the pain, the confusion, the anger and the fear – it all came spilling out.

He just listened.

When I had finished talking he stared at me in horrible silence.

'I think you're the bravest person I've ever met,' he finally said. 'I love you.'

Chapter 22

The Woman in the Mirror

The bellboy was already unloading our suitcases by the time we stepped out of the blue taxi. His smart maroon uniform emblazoned with gold buttons looked slightly out of place in the sizzling heat.

The staccato clack of my stiletto heels echoed off the cool marble floor in the hotel lobby.

It was dim inside. Even the 16 bulbs of the glistening crystal chandelier couldn't compete with the glare of the afternoon sun.

A pretty girl in traditional Thai dress approached us with a tray of fruit cocktails, 'A welcome drink, sir and madam.'

I took it gratefully, sipping through a straw decorated with little sprigs of white jasmine.

The receptionist greeted us with a cheery smile. 'Mr and Mrs Tormey, welcome.'

Kevin and I grinned at each other. We were still getting used to hearing ourselves referred to as that.

'We have you booked into a superior double suite with a city-view balcony. Is that all correct?'

I smiled a yes.

'Wonderful. Here is your key card, Mrs Tormey. You'll find a bottle of complimentary champagne waiting in your room. Enjoy your stay.'

I took the key and followed the bellboy towards the elevator.

The bedroom was huge, with a king-size bed laid out with pristine white sheets and fluffy pillows. In the bathroom was a massive circular bath clad in grey veined marble. I stared at my reflection in the mirror. Here it was. Proof of how far I had come.

Gone was the scraggly haired, skinny little girl who was scared of her own shadow. This tall, attractive and confident woman staring back at me had replaced her. This woman dressed in smart clothes with a made-up face and glossy long chestnut-brown tresses; a woman with a successful career in Human Resources; a woman with her gorgeous new husband about to honeymoon in a five-star hotel. I had to smile and pull silly faces at my reflection to convince myself that the woman looking back at me really was me.

The pop of the cork startled me for a second.

'Champagne, my gorgeous wife,' said Kevin, flashing his huge smile. 'Happy honeymoon.'

He opened the bedroom door and stepped out onto the balcony of our room. The sounds of the city drifted up to our eighth-floor room. It was unmistakably Bangkok – tuk-tuks, traffic horns, street vendors shouting out their wares, and the low hum of motorbikes.

For years that noise had filled me with absolute fear – it was the sound of the Antichrist. I chuckled at the thought and stepped out onto the balcony to join Kevin.

We toasted our future happiness and kissed for a few

minutes before taking in the view. A sprawling mass of urban humanity spread out before us; the people and cars down below looked tiny as ants.

'Can you see your old neighbourhood from here?' he asked, one arm around my waist.

The question threw me.

'Actually,' I started with a laugh, 'I've honestly got no idea. We lived in Bangkok, but not really "in" Bangkok. It was like a prison, really. Apart from the odd day out to perform or witness, all I saw was barbed wire and high gates. It might as well have been Mars.' I let out a wry laugh. 'If they had told me we *did* live on Mars I probably would have believed them.'

Given my childhood history Thailand may seem like a strange place to want to spend my honeymoon. But I needed Kevin to see it and for him to have a sense of where I grew up. Coming back here with my new husband felt like fitting together another piece of the jigsaw puzzle that was my life.

We had married on Réunion island. Returning there as Kevin's bride had felt triumphantly fantastic. For the first time in my life I was doing something that made me feel proud. I wore orchids in my hair and a strapless flowing white dress which made me feel like a princess. My sister Aimée, now 18 years old, was my bridesmaid. Some of my brothers had flown in for the occasion. It was the first proper family reunion we'd had in years.

As I prepared to walk through the garden on my father's arm his voice cracked with emotion. 'You look beautiful, my darling girl. I pray you two will have a blessed and wonderful marriage.'

Even my mother managed to say the right things.

'Natacha, I hope you and Kevin are truly happy together as your father and I have been. I am praying for you both.'

Kevin looked dashing in an open-necked shirt and linen suit as he waited for me at the front of the pagoda they'd had specially erected for the ceremony.

As the music started and my father and I walked towards him, my mother, brothers and sister Aimée turned to face us. I was filled with love for Kevin and excitement at marrying him. And the wonderful sense of family intimacy and belonging made the whole thing incredibly special. After all the years of hardship, of anger and of being separated from my family, either physically or emotionally, here we were together at last. It was as if I had finally found what I had been missing for so long.

It wasn't lost on me what an influence this was on my more troubled siblings too. I was now living proof that an upbringing like ours could be surmounted. I'd spent my life locked behind a commune wall, had barely any education, endured beatings and abuse, yet I had finally achieved success – if a decent job, a home and a happy life can be how success is measured.

As we sat down for our post-wedding meal I winced as my father said grace. I know lots of families say grace before eating, so it's not that unusual, but ours was about the cult so it was embarrassing to me.

'Lord, we thank you for this food that you have provided and we pray that you bless us and our family worldwide and our dear Queen Maria. We love you, Jesus.'

For much of the rest of the week we stayed with them I was on edge. The house was full of cult-related literature and Mo letters. I was terrified Kevin might pick something up and start reading it, but he's not a big reader at the best of times and to my relief I don't think he even noticed it. If he did then he was too polite to say anything.

Despite all the stories he'd heard from me I was thankful Kevin didn't judge my parents. Towards the end of our trip he even took my father out to the local betting shop to place a bet on the European Cup final. My dad had always said gambling was a strictly forbidden sin, so I couldn't believe Kevin persuaded him to go along. When they came back they were both laughing at a silly joke. I was so grateful to Kevin for normalising what could have been a really weird situation.

At the end of our stay they both told me that they approved of him. I know it shouldn't really have mattered if they didn't, but I can't deny I was pleased.

The whole thing had been a bit like a dream. By the time we arrived in Thailand we were exhausted. The champagne went straight to our heads so we went to bed. We woke up at 3 a.m. starving and ordered room service. We sat in bed eating a Thai feast and giggling. I freaked out when I spilled chilli sauce on the bed and ran off to get a cloth to wash it off.

'Leave it. It's a hotel.' Kevin laughed at me. 'We're paying for the privilege. They'll change it in the morning.'

My mood went instantly darker. 'There was a time when so much as getting up to go to the loo got me a beating, Kevin. I'm not quite at the full decadence stage yet.'

That incident threw me and I went back to sleep feeling very out of sorts. I had a terrible nightmare in which it was the End Time. I was stranded with a group of people on a roof; there were massive floods below us. I was aware that I had survived the flood but I knew I was about to die. I woke up sweating and overcome with a dreadful feeling of desperation and resignation.

I went into the bathroom and held my head against the cool marble wall. Fear rushed over me like a wave. What if my dream was a prophecy? A glimpse of the future?

My heart started to race.

Dreams like that are a familiar pattern to me. Since leaving the cult I have at least one a week. I have learned to talk myself down by reminding myself it's not real, just a remnant of the twisted doctrines I was fed for so long.

At breakfast I still felt a bit unsettled. We decided to go for a walk round the city.

As we exited the hotel a tuk-tuk buzzed right past like a giant bumblebee. Vendors and shopkeepers waved and shouted at us as we walked along the street hand in hand.

'No thanks, mate.'

Kevin was working full time to keep them at bay.

A waft of grilled chicken and the distinctive aroma of peanut sauce caught in my nostrils. We'd only just finished eating breakfast, but the smell was so good it tugged at my taste buds.

'Mmmm. That looks amazing,' said Kevin, lingering to stare at the little grill with skewers of meat on it.

I nodded towards a pile of rubbish next to the food stall. Three large brown rats crawled over it.

'You don't seriously think ...?' said Kevin, staring from rats to grill.

'Gross. Let's hope not,' I chuckled.

'Whatever. Slap enough peanut sauce on it, would you really care?'

We both burst out laughing.

My Thailand was not this vibrant place of fun, colour, noise and smells. My Thailand had been a prison – drab, authoritarian, paranoid and dystopian. I had lived in fear of an outside world I was led to believe was corrupt and evil, filled with disbelieving 'systemites' and Antichrist soldiers who wanted to kill me.

But now, strolling along with Kevin, I was almost completely relaxed. I'll admit, part of me was slightly on edge, but I realised that Bangkok, with its hawkers, greedy taxi drivers and pickpockets, has that effect on many tourists. And that's what I was now – just an average tourist. It felt brilliant.

A few days later we headed out of the city for the beach, checking into a fabulous hotel built on a cliff overlooking the sea. The décor was antique Thai-style, all carved dark wood and brightly coloured rich silks. In the evening we ate at a little beach restaurant with tables set out on the sand. As I watched the sunset over the sparkling Andaman Sea I recalled my childhood day on the beach with Leah, baby Thérèse, my mom and four big brothers. It's probably the only memory I have where we were allowed to behave like children, full of laughter and rowdiness. In the years that followed we became so oppressed and in fear of violence that we stopped laughing loudly or playing too boisterously. We were constantly on edge, adjusting to ever-changing rules and trying to avoid the next beating.

'What's up? Turn that frown upside down. We're on holiday.' Kevin had spotted my dark cloud.

I smiled across the table at him. When I first began to fall in love with him I liked to imagine we were like Adam and Eve in the Garden of Eden, two lovers in perfect paradise.

Then I moved in, and his house became our home. It was just like the houses I had gazed at so longingly from the train window after I first moved to London – modern red brick with a neat front lawn and Kevin's Mercedes parked in the driveway. The back garden became my own version of Eden. Digging and planting gave me a sense of order. I loved the sensation of getting soil under my fingernails and creating beauty out of nothing. The ability to shoot weeds with lightning bolts might have been handy, but my trowel did the same job.

Out in my garden was where I felt safest, happiest and calmest. I could go to the toilet without having to ask permission, go to the kitchen and get a glass of water or make a sandwich whenever I felt thirsty or hungry. And when I was done gardening I could lock myself in the shower, soaking my body with hot water and scented shower gel, before getting dressed in smart new clothes that fitted me properly.

The ordinariness of it all was everything I had ever wanted.

But, just like Adam and Eve, there was a fall.

All the happiness, the sense of love and safety, the life I'd always dreamed of and the chance of fulfilment – somehow all these good things conspired in the back of my mind. They took me over. I felt unworthy, like an undeserving impostor. I could not come to grips with being happy. Worse than that, some dark part of my psyche had crawled forth to actively sabotage my well-being.

I felt so safe with Kevin, but at times I struggled with intimacy. Sometimes during sex I would have a panic attack and be unable to breathe, pushing him off me. Afterwards I wouldn't let him come near me or touch me.

On one occasion, just after I had moved in, Kevin made a sudden movement to get something off the kitchen shelf and I panicked, cowering and covering my head with my hands to protect myself. The sad, hurt look in his eyes was unbearable as he gently lifted my arms back down and gave me a cuddle. 'Oh babe, I'd never hit you. How could you think that?' My reaction was an instinctive reflex, a legacy of so many beatings.

The thought of having kids one day filled me with terror. Even though I had spent years looking after my younger siblings and knew I could do it all practically, I began to convince myself that my past would make me an unfit mother. All sorts of dark thoughts whizzed around my head. What if I hit them? What if I couldn't show them affection? What if I went mad and thought the world was ending?

As our relationship went on I became increasingly paranoid that Kevin was being unfaithful to me. I would check his mobile phone and hack into his email account looking for messages from other lovers. Finding nothing didn't reassure me; it only served to make me more convinced he was lying. So I dreamed up even more bizarre ways to catch him out by setting traps for him – tests to search for any evidence of infidelity. I would plant condoms in the pockets of his coat and then count them to see if he'd used any. It was insane.

Enduring my paranoia was so testing for him. Most other men would have left me. I think it speaks volumes about his genuine warmth and empathy that he could see that my erratic behaviour was a product of my upbringing. And, more than being able to understand my behaviour, he managed to see past it, to me. He could see past all the dark moods, the mistrust, the need to control, the fear and the paranoia – and still see clearly enough to love me, despite myself.

Little by little we found a way to bridge the difficulties together. For example, sometimes his work takes him away for a few days. The first few times it happened I got so anxious at being left on my own that I had panic attacks, clutching at the walls and gasping for breath. I bombarded him with needy text messages. When he came back I glossed over it all and pretended everything was normal, getting dinner ready and making myself look pretty – all the things I thought 'normal' women did.

But of course he could see right through it. And he gently explained to me how hard it was for him to be on the receiving end of all that crazy paranoia when he was trying to work.

So we developed a little system where we mark the calendar weeks in advance when he's going to be away. I calm myself by checking the calendar and telling myself I will be fine if I get prepared. I make sure I plan fun activities for myself or invite a friend round to keep me company, so that by the time Kevin leaves I am not in a state of hyper-anxiety. For his part he checks in with me regularly so my imagination doesn't start to run away with me.

Being super-organised keeps me calmer. I make lists for just about everything because planning ahead stops me feeling terrified about things going wrong. For example, if I need to take a train journey to a place I have never been before, I write down two or three different possible journey routes just in case. I can see that for some people this level of attention to detail might be exhausting, but for me it works because it keeps my mind rational.

The slightest thing can send me spiralling into a panic attack – someone accidentally bumping into me on the street, the smell of Dettol. I live in fear of the triggers that lurk around every corner.

But even though I can mitigate some of the symptoms I know I'll never be entirely free of them. Depression and anxiety are things I have had to learn to live with. They are like the constant nagging voices in my head. I battle them and I try to keep them at bay, but the best way to do that is to accept they will be my companions through life. I have to accept them, get to know them and occasionally let them in when they threaten to knock my emotional doors down.

When I get stressed I pick at my nails. Other friends who grew up in the cult tell me they pick at their skull or hair or have developed alopecia.

I have had counselling, and that has helped, but there have been times when I think even my counsellor can't understand the things I've been through and struggles to know what to say to me. So many of my childhood stories are just so off the scale.

I still carry a large bag. These days it has make-up and keys, the normal things all women carry in their handbag. But I still also have my first aid kit and the torch – old habits die hard. I managed to wean myself off the compass because even I could see how ridiculous it was to carry a compass on the train to work. But even now that inbred fear of disaster or belief that I might need to suddenly hide from the Antichrist still runs very deep.

Kevin took a leap of faith in marrying me. That wasn't lost on me, and I knew I had to repay that trust by showing I could learn to trust him back.

After dinner we sat on our balcony, drinking. We had been playing a silly game where we were only allowed to talk in the other one's voice and use their mannerisms. Kevin had sent up my control-freak tendencies mercilessly, but instead of being a tearful, hurt, gibbering wreck as I once would have been, I was laughing so hard my sides hurt. Surely being able to laugh at oneself is one of the most healing things there is?

The night was hot and sticky. I couldn't sleep. As Kevin snored quietly I padded back out onto the terrace and sat there lost in my thoughts. By the time the sun rose up over the sea my mind was clear. I knew what I needed to do.

I took out a pen and paper and wrote a letter to my brother Marc.

In it I told him how much I missed him and loved him. I told him all about Kevin and how happy I was. I said I knew that he and Kevin would have got on really well and how much that pleased me. I also told him what a wonderful husband and father he would have been had he lived and how unfair it was that he never got the chance to fulfil all of his own dreams.

I told him about the rose garden I had begun planting for him at home. I had bought the first one not long after I moved in – a scented yellow bloom. I told him how I planned to plant one for each of his 27 years. That way I can have something to look at when I think of him, and I have created something beautiful, fragile and alive – just as he was.

I ended my letter by promising Marc I would honour his memory by living for the both of us. And that he would be in my thoughts every day for the rest of my life. He was loved and never forgotten. My inspiration for not giving up.

I took my carefully folded letter and poked it through the neck of an empty wine bottle.

When Kevin woke up I told him my plan and we took a little ferry to a nearby island. I stood on the deck, silent in my private world of grief. Once we were in the middle of the sea I whispered a prayer before tossing the bottle into the water, where it bobbed on the surface, swirling around in the swell left by the boat.

I felt Kevin come and stand behind me. The bottle bobbed once more, then disappeared beneath the waves.

I turned to my husband.

'I never want to come here again. I want to go home.'

Epilogue

Buckinghamshire, 2014

The sun glints through my conservatory window as my cat Athena plays at my feet. My husband is in the kitchen cooking dinner. I'm tired after a long day at the office and wondering what to watch on TV tonight.

On the way home from work I went to the supermarket, and as I was loading my shopping bags in the car I burst out laughing. I couldn't stop. I had this crazy burst of joy where I suddenly realised just how absurd it is to be so thrilled at having such an ordinary, average lifestyle. The little tasks in life that most people find boring – such as shopping for groceries or loading up the car with petrol – are things I really love because they are a sign of the normality I never imagined I'd have.

Very few people know my history. It's not the kind of thing you can just drop into the conversation. Generally when I meet a new person my fake life story goes like this: I was born and raised in Thailand because my father worked for the French Embassy in Bangkok. Despite being French, I have a North American accent because I learned my English in international schools. I come from such a large family of siblings because my parents are old fashioned and Catholic, but we are close and all get along wonderfully.

I hate lying, but what choice do I have? How could people understand my life? I am still struggling to make sense of it myself.

The cult still exists and is known today as The Family International. They have rebranded themselves to come across as a slick, glossy international evangelical Christian organisation. Karen Zerby (Mama Maria) is still its leader, although she has changed her name by deed poll to Katherine Smith. No one knows her exact whereabouts but she's highly visible on the Internet, writing blogs about faith. Recently I saw one she wrote about motherhood – this is the same woman whose son Davidito was driven into insanity and murder.

Sara, the author of *The Story of Davidito*, is allegedly still a senior member and leader of the cult. She has never been called to account for authoring the book. Her daughter Davida struggled for many years after leaving the cult, and worked as an exotic dancer in the USA. She has given several highly articulate television interviews denouncing the cult and talking about the terrible abuse she and Davidito suffered while growing up in Berg's household. Yet the cult has dismissed poor Davida as a liar.

I don't know what finally became of tragic Mene.

On my Bangkok honeymoon I met up with Claire, my old friend and the sister of disabled James. She told me that poor James had finally been put out of his misery and died when he was 18. He collapsed in the shower one day, unable to get up. Claire thinks he may have had a stroke but isn't really sure. She too has since left the cult, and we remain good friends today.

The cult committed horrible crimes against children. To this day The Family have got away with it because how can victims like me ever bring legal cases against our abusers when we don't even know their real names? I don't know if Clay is still alive. If so, I wonder if he is haunted with guilt for the crimes he committed against me? Or does he continue to abuse children today?

A couple of years ago I discovered that when Clay had disappeared from our commune back when I was little it was because my father had him excommunicated after discovering he had abused another girl. I recall how terrified I was that Clay would come back and hurt me. If I had been told he had gone for good and why, it would have helped me so much. I might even have found my voice and spoken up about my abuse. And although excommunicating him was at least something, it didn't punish him or stop him being free to go on and abuse other kids. He should have been reported to the police, but of course that would never have happened because protecting the cult's reputation was all that mattered to the adult members. It mattered more to them than the lives of the children ever did. That thought disgusts me to my core.

My siblings have fared variously: some are in denial, others are angry and traumatised. Most of us have battled, or still do, with depression and anxiety. The demons are always there, like a dark cloud threatening to burst at any moment. But we try to move forward and make the most of the lives that we have built for ourselves.

Joe, the eldest, rarely talks about the years he spent in Teen Training Camp. But I have learned, mostly through other ex-members' accounts, that it was a place filled with horrors. The youngsters at the camp were forced to do hard labour, not allowed to talk for days at a time and badly beaten. Joe stayed longer in The Family than any of us, but is out of the group today.

Matt still lives with Sienna, his long-time partner, and their three children in France. He's still the same funny entertainer he always was, but he has a dark side too. The sarcasm and jokes are an act to cover up his pain, but he can never fool me because I see all too clearly my own anguish mirrored in his eyes.

Vincent, so misunderstood as a child and probably the victim of the worst violence, has had an ongoing battle with depression. He struggled with addictions when he was younger, but he's truly turned his life around since. He and his husband recently moved to Cyprus, where he works in the financial services industry. I love him so very much and still try to protect him like I have always done. Earlier this year I was thinking about it all and the ways it has affected us. I started to think about Vincent and the violence they meted out to him. He hasn't ever had counselling, partly because it can be so expensive. The thought of that made me angry, so angry that I became deeply depressed. I emailed Karen Zerby (Mama Maria), using the contact email on the now very glossy and professional-looking Family International website. I had heard they had recently set up a fund to help elderly members. So I wrote to ask why they hadn't also set aside money to help the children they and their members abused. In my mind they should be supporting second-generation children like Vincent by paying for counselling.

This is my letter:

Buckinghamshire, 2014

Dear Maria,

I am a second-generation ex-member of The Family International and I am writing to you to put in a request on behalf of my brother. I do not wish to play blame games or get into matters of the past. However, as the balanced individual I have become since I left the cult I do believe that people who made errors of judgement which resulted in people or children being abused and damaged should try to take steps to remedy the past.

My brothers and I were physically, emotionally and sexually abused during our childhood in Bangkok homes. As I said, I do not want to go into details as it is pointless but my brother has struggled with depression as a result of the traumatic events in his childhood.

To get to the point of my email, I heard some of TFI's fortune will be distributed to members over a certain age. I was wondering why a portion of that has not been set aside to help ex-members who need specialised counselling or psychological help to get over their past? Surely as The Family has acknowledged that some of Berg's writings caused an environment that allowed for abuse to occur then they should have, long ago, demonstrated their desire to help those affected by that? The purpose of this email is to officially apply for funding that will allow my brother to get the help he needs so our family can stand a chance at becoming normal and avoid another tragedy as a result of the group's doctrines.

He did not have a choice. He was born into a lifestyle that destroyed him, unlike other FGIs who joined out of choice.

Thank you for considering my request.

I waited over six months for a reply.

November 18, 2013
Dear Natacha,
We hope this finds you well and in good health. We're sorry it has taken a while to get back to you on your letter. We were attempting to investigate the background on the situation, since we are not personally familiar with it, but we were unable to do so. As you may know, in 2010, TFI restructured, which resulted in the virtual dismantling of the communal households, the prior leadership structure, and the boards. At this time, TFI operates in many ways as a virtual network.

You didn't mention where your brother lived, and whether he had been able to research what possibilities are available to him within the medical system of the country he is living in. If he is in England, there are public healthcare avenues open to him from what we understand, as there apparently are in a number of other EU countries. We're not sure if there are other factors or if he has already been able to research options to receive funding for counselling or consultation with a psychologist or other professional, as you were saying he needed.

We don't know if you have already communicated this need with your parents and whether they are able to help in researching help for your brother and we would like to suggest that this may be an option.

We are very sorry to hear that you feel that your brother was mistreated during his time growing up in The Family. We believe that every child deserves a happy and safe environment for growing up, and to this end we instituted numerous policies in the Charter and developed child protection policies. We are saddened to hear that these policies did not provide you and your brother the nurturing environment they were intended to ensure. To any Family member or former Family member who feels he or she has suffered any mistreatment of any kind, by anyone, we are truly sorry.

In 2008, TFI issued an open apology to current and former second-generation members in which leadership apologised to any second-generation member who, due to the lack of restrictions and stringent child protection policies from 1978 through the mid-1980s, was subjected to hurtful or harmful behavior of any kind (http://www.myconclusion.com/apology-to-second-generation). An apology was also published in 2009, which we encourage you to read, if you haven't already done so. (It can be accessed here: www.myconclusion.com/category/letters-of-apology.)

We want to reiterate our heartfelt apologies to you, Natacha, and your brother for any hurt or difficulties either of you faced. We are very sorry for any pain or unhappiness you and your brother experienced during your years in The Family.

In regards to your financial request, we regret that we are not able to disburse funds from the Veteran Missionary Care fund for purposes other than that for which the fund was designated, which is for aging members. The fund is minimal and will provide a small one-time stipend for elder members. We wish that TFI had funding to assist all members and former members of all ages, but regrettably, finances are very limited and since the Reboot, with people transitioning, there is little structure or finances available. We're truly sorry about this.

Again, please accept our apologies for this late response. Our prayers are with your brother, that he is able to find healing and closure. We wish you all the best, and hope that your life will be filled with peace and fulfillment.

Best regards,
Carol Cunningham
For TFI Public Affairs

I don't really know what I expected. I never believed they would help, but their reply still left me staggered with its cold corporate professionalism. The public apology they refer to was half-hearted at best. The leadership didn't admit responsibility for anything; instead they sought to blame the systematic and widespread abuse on the actions of a few rogue individuals.

Despite all that has happened to my parents they are still madly in love and very happily married. They have recently left the cult and returned to France, where they survive on a combination of state welfare and whatever seasonal work they can find.

The system that they once hated and feared is now their only ally because the cult will not help those people whom they used for decades. They devoted their entire lives to The Family but in the end it spat them out without a penny to their name. My dad is now in his late fifties and has just started looking for his first full-time job.

The younger ones missed the worst years of commune living so were not as badly affected, but they still suffer in their own ways.

Buckinghamshire, 2014

My half-sister, Thérèse, is living in France with her mother, Leah, who divorced Uncle Edward. She and my parents are great friends again and visit each other regularly. Thérèse remains a quiet and reserved character. She has been to visit me in England and I'm also very happy for her that she has my father back in her life.

Andy, Chris, Louis, Laurent and Brian live at home with my parents.

I adore my younger siblings and, despite the past, I still love my parents. I have visited them a couple of times since they have moved to Europe and I am finally at peace with the past and where we are now. At times our relationship is strained, and we go through periods where communication is impossible. I sadly accept it will always be that way, and it pains me that even now the cult's vile influence continues to cause conflict within our family.

And I do still have many unanswered questions for my mother and father.

I find it difficult to understand how they and thousands of other adults were brainwashed so severely that they could not see the perverse sexual doctrines and behaviours of their leaders. How on earth could their dedication to the cult be so deep for them to put their loyalty to it above the well-being of their own children? I look back with absolute horror at their absences in our early years and the cold emotional rejection they showed my brothers and me when we left the group.

A few years ago I asked my father if he regretted the past. He told me he did regret going on a 'spiritual journey with small children in tow' because he could see now that it was selfish. But strangely he couldn't yet express regret for himself or recognise himself as a victim of the cult.

I also asked him if he had his time over whether he'd choose to do it all again. He said he couldn't go there or even allow himself to think about the question. Heartbreakingly, he said the hardest thing of all for him is the fact he is still in this world. He didn't expect to be an old man of retirement age still struggling to feed his kids in a harsh 'system' world. He and my mother were promised a martyr's paradise – the gold mansions and singing lakes of heaven that were depicted in the posters on the commune walls. Both of them still live with the fear that the sky is going to fall in on their heads and worry that by leaving the group they have somehow angered God.

I was just 18 when I escaped the cult. I had my whole life in front of me. But my parents were fed those lies their entire adult life. They gave their whole lives away, sacrificing their careers, money and lifestyle. Yet the leadership has never had the decency to confess the truth and admit they failed their followers. For me that would have been the least they could have done. They lied to people whose lives were in their hands.

I accept that my parents were brainwashed and are as much victims of the cult as I am. Brainwashing is more powerful than people realise. Over the years the victim is stripped of their individuality, becoming a ghost of who they once were. They are reprogrammed to believe the doctrines of their manipulator, losing their bearings on what is right and wrong. Any natural instinct towards their real family is simply replaced by devotion to the cult.

Breaking free is only the beginning. Then begins the painful process of reversing the indoctrination. The longer someone stays in a cult the harder it is for them to remember who they were before the cult took control of their mind. Or in the case of someone like me, a cult-born child, my entire personality was made and created by them. When I left I had no idea who I was. My whole existence, everything I thought I knew, had been a lie.

But it is the psychological aftermath of life in a cult that is all too often the silent killer.

To date there have been approximately 40 suicides of ex-Children of God members, most of them not adult members like my parents, but the second generation like me who were born into the cult – the innocents who had no control over their fate.

Author's Note

For those of you who left this world because the pain was too much to bear, know that we have finally exposed them for what they are. This book is for you – the nameless, voiceless children of the cult. You will always be my family.

Born into the CHILDREN OF GOD